# 'Made in Scotland'

## Household Names that Began in Scotland

Carol Foreman

BIRLINN

To Mum

We miss you more than we
ever thought possible

First published in 2004
Second edition published in 2010 by
Birlinn Limited
West Newington House
10 Newington Road
Edinburgh EH9 1QS
www.birlinn.co.uk

ISBN 978 1 84158 725 7

British Library Cataloguing-in-Publication Data
A catalogue record for this book is available
from the British Library

Typeset in Gill Sans light
Design: Mark Blackadder

Printed and bound by
Bell & Bain Ltd, Glasgow

# INTRODUCTION

Of the wide range and diversity of British products in the marketplace, both at home and abroad, the Scots can take pride in the fact that many of them began in Scotland and are now household names. For example, Dr E. J. Mills, a chemist at the Royal Technical College, Glasgow, invented that well-known bleach Parozone in 1891. When people around the world spread Robertson's 'Golden Shred' marmalade on their toast, it is courtesy of Paisley man James Robertson and his wife, Marion. How would cooks thicken their sauces easily without cornflour, first produced in Paisley by Brown & Polson in 1854?

The world's first concentrated bottled fruit drink was Rose's Lime Juice Cordial, invented by Leith man Lachlan Rose. The finest shortbread in the world is produced by Walkers of Aberlour, and the UK's No. 1 comic, *The Beano*, is published in Dundee. The world's best-selling Scotch whisky is Johnnie Walker Red Label, bottled in Kilmarnock. Glenfiddich Distillery in Dufftown produces the world's best-selling malt whisky. Dewar & Sons' Aberfeldy Distillery produces the

biggest selling scotch whisky in the US. Scotland's 'Other National Drink', Irn-Bru, is an international brand that began in the Gallowgate in Glasgow in 1901. On the bottled water front, Highland Spring in Perthshire is the UK's No. 1 sparkling water brand.

Pringle of Hawick gave the world the knitted twin-set, and J & P Coats of Paisley, whose origins go back to 1830, grew to become the largest thread manufacturer in the world. In the bathroom, the Shanks part of the internationally known Armitage Shanks refers to John Shanks of Paisley.

*Made in Scotland* features the stories behind forty household names that began in Scotland, most of which have stood the test of time. Some that have not, however, such as British Caledonian Airways and Templeton Carpets, are fondly remembered and appear in the section entitled 'Gone, But Not Forgotten'.

Many of the stories behind the contributions to daily life given to us by Scots are fascinating, as they are those of enterprising young people who achieved their aims, not by plentiful funds but through the

Scottish virtues of hard work, perseverance, integrity, courage and initiative. While they all began their business lives in a small way or by chance, against all the odds they were successful, like William Younger, who laid the foundations of what became the brewery giant Scottish & Newcastle, now named Heineken UK. Among Scottish institutions, The Royal Bank of Scotland, established in 1727, grew into the fifth largest bank in the world.

While, sadly, some of the brands featured in *Made in Scotland* have been taken over by multi-national companies and are no longer manufactured in Scotland, others are still being manufactured in the land of their birth. Some are even owned, or are being managed by, descendants of the founders.

Apart from being a compilation of famous brands that began in Scotland and a salute to Scottish industry and the remarkable people who made it great, *Made in Scotland* is a nostalgic journey into the past. The many illustrations give a chance to see again the old advertisements, slogans and trademarks of the products featured.

# CONTENTS

The name Armitage Shanks is ubiquitous in the world of bathrooms, and millions of people use one of its products every day. The company came about when two long established companies, one named after a place and the other after a person, amalgamated. The place is Armitage in Staffordshire and the person is John Shanks. For our purposes it is the Shanks part of the Armitage Shanks' story that we are interested in.

John Shanks was born in Paisley in 1825, the son of a handloom weaver. He was apprenticed as a

John Shanks

plumber to Wallace and Connell of Glasgow, and then worked as a journeyman plumber in the Paisley area until, aged 30, he started his own plumbing business in Barrhead, seven miles from Glasgow.

Being an innovative man, John Shanks began to devise improvements to sanitary ware, and in 1863 his first patent was for a trapless water closet, the 'Patent Flexible Valve Closet' as he called it, but which was known in the work's catalogue as 'Number Four'. Sales nationwide brought success to the company, and in 1871 when the Prince of Wales was dangerously ill with typhoid, investigations showed that every sanitary device in Buckingham Palace was defective except the Shanks 'Number Four' in the servants' quarters.

In 1875, John and his brother Andrew, also a plumber, founded Shanks and Co. Sanitary Engineers. About this time, to manufacture the fittings for John's various inventions, the company also opened a small brass foundry that was the start of the famous Tubal Works. These were named after the Old Testament figure Tubal Cain, the first worker in brass and iron.

In 1877 John took out a patent for delivering water to basins through side inlets. A similar design was used in the 1880s on the company's Citizen washbasins and Imperial baths. Only the spindle and knobs of the tap were exposed and

Above left. A John Shanks' patent of 1892 – his 'modern' bath.
Above right. Water closets featured in Shanks' 1895 catalogue.

the water entered the basin through small perforations in the earthenware. Basins were sometimes fitted with a hair-washing apparatus

In 1884 Shanks exhibited the 'Eureka' canopy bath at the International Health exhibition in South Kensington. It was fitted with the full range of shower effects and was enclosed in an elegant wooden cabinet. The 'Eureka' was described as 'the acme of luxurious bathing'. By the mid-1880s, Shanks advertised their 'Patent Pedestal Bidet', with hot and cold water and an ascending spray, claiming it was 'a very necessary appliance in a well appointed bathroom'. This continental appliance, however, was little-understood and even mistrusted in Britain and America.

By the 1890s the firm occupied a seven-acre site and employed 600 men. By 1894 John had taken out around 100 patents and the company had established itself as Britain's leader in sanitary engineering.

Shanks' products were to be found in hospitals, public buildings and households throughout Britain. Nearer home, the firm designed equipment for Glasgow's Western Infirmary and Paisley Infirmary.

John Shanks died in December 1895, after which his son John and his nephew William carried on the business. John always looked after his employees, providing in his will an extra day's pay to those who had been with the company for six months on the day of his death.

After John's death the company continued to flourish, and around 1900 the Victoria Pottery was established to ensure uniformity of quality and economy in production.

At the same time a showroom was opened at 81 Bond Street London to allow for a larger share of the West End trade.

Shanks' business was not confined to Britain; it exported

Armitage Shanks' advertisement c1984 advertising the exclusive Dolphin range that revives the days of traditional Victorian splendour.

overseas, ensuring an international reputation, and in 1897 it supplied the Melbourne Metropolitan Board of Works with 8,000 cisterns to be used throughout the city. In 1909, 15,000 cisterns were shipped to Argentina, followed a year later by an order for a further 22,000. All the British colonies were supplied.

When it came to supplying fittings for passenger liners, Shanks was the first choice, and among other ships their products were fitted in the *Mauritania, Lusitania* and the *Titanic*. Much later it installed sanitary equipment throughout the *Queen Elizabeth*.

The firm was run by the Shanks family until 1969, when it merged with Armitage Ware to form Armitage Shanks. The Armitage part of the business was founded in 1817 by Thomas Bond in Armitage, Staffordshire. In 1980 Armitage Shanks became a member of the Blue Circle Industries Group. In 1992 the Barrhead factory closed, and today, Armitage Shanks is a brand of Ideal Standard International Brands.

Shanks' Siphonic Closet advertised in 1896 in *The Bailie Magazine*

Although Askit powders are a household name, most people would be surprised to discover that they originated in Glasgow and go back to the early 1900s when Adam Laidlaw and his wife opened a small apothecary's shop in Keppochhill Road on the north side of the city. As at the time it was common for customers to ask apothecaries to prescribe cures for lesser ailments such as colds, flu, hangovers, etc, Mr Laidlaw devised an APC (aspirin, phenacetin, caffeine) powder that he sold as an effective relief for headaches, colds, flu, neuralgia, neuritis, arthritis and all nerve pains — in fact, a panacea. He maintained that his proportions plus the use of caffeine citrate (not alkali) and the addition of an antacid, magnesium trisilicate, held the secret of his product's success. Over two years, 300 to 650 powders per week were sold to Mr Laidlaw's customers.

At the end of the First World War, Mr and Mrs Laidlaw employed a young accountant, John McRobbie Low, to act as their financial adviser. John had returned from the war and had resumed his career with a Glasgow firm of chartered accountants.

Shortly after appointing John Low, Mr Laidlaw felt he was becoming too old to give his product the support it deserved. He therefore asked his young accountant if he would take it and do something with it. As John Low agreed with Mr Laidlaw about the product's potential, his answer was 'yes' and in 1920 a manufacturing company was created. Apart from finding finance, however, there were a couple of other problems to be addressed. One was that, as 600 powders per week was the maximum number that could be weighed and packed by hand, some form of mechanical device would have to be designed to produce the same product in the same pack as before but in far greater quantities at much higher speeds. The second problem was that the product had no specific name. This however, was solved when two young girls wanting to buy an obviously personal item entered the shop with

Photograph taken in 1945 of the Askit factory in Saracen Street with the workforce on parade.

An Askit advertisement that appeared in *The Bulletin* newspaper of 11 December 1936. The company advertised prolifically in the press as well as on buses, railway station signs, hoardings and theatre curtains and in theatre programmes.

diffidence. One said to the other, 'If it's the lady chemist, I'll ask it, if it's the man chemist you ask it.' In the Glasgow dialect the 'a' is narrow, as in 'arrow', and the word 'for' is omitted. Mrs Laidlaw, who was in the back shop at the time, heard the conversation and immediately felt she had found the perfect name for her husband's analgesic powders – Askit. The next day the name was registered and the Askit Manufacturing Company was born.

Askit Manufacturing moved into a purpose-built building in Saracen Street, Possilpark, in 1920, which was opened by Lord Provost Swan of Glasgow. At this point, those involved in Askit Manufacturing decided to form a limited company and, on 13 April 1925, Askit Limited was incorporated. By the mid-1940s the company was employing around forty workers and producing around twenty million powders a year compared to 20,000 in 1920. In the 1950s, a selling organisation in Canada was established to meet the demands of Scots exiles there, and in Toronto alone thousands of Askit powders were sold every month. Askit powders also found their way to Europe, Africa, Malaya, New Zealand and Australia, to name just a few places.

Right from the start, Askit was not shy in advertising. It knew it had a first-class analgesic product that 'cured' headaches, colds, flu and all nerve pains, and it was not afraid to say so. It used all the advertising media available at the time – the press, buses, railway station signs, hoardings and theatre curtains – all of which had the slogan 'Is there an Askit in the house?' Theatre programmes also carried Askit advertisements and 65 per cent of

Askit label of 1939 which stated that Askit was 'absolutely safe', a statement that is not allowed todayas advertising restrictions and controls advocate that everything has to becredible, and 'beyond belief' and the old Askit wording implied the incredible.

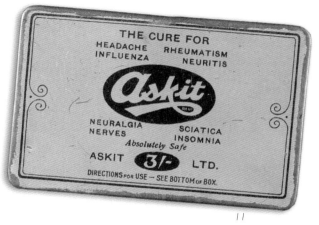

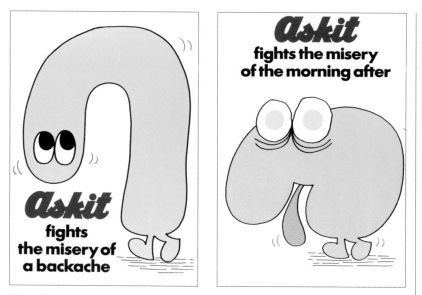

Two of the popular and humorous Askit Miseries advertisements which ran from 1971 to 1994.

Scottish buses carried the slogan 'Askit, the safe remedy'. All advertisements carried the additional message 'Powders 3d and 1/6d'.

While in Askit's early years all advertising was relatively free from restrictions and controls, in the late 1960s restrictions were introduced. In Askit's case the phrase 'Relief beyond belief' was rated as unacceptable as statements had to be credible, and 'beyond belief' implied the incredible. Similarly, 'An Askit tonight, tomorrow all right' indicated a speed of action in a medicine that was not allowed. The words 'safe' and 'cures' were banned.

In view of the restrictions, a complete change of Askit advertising had to be found, and as at that time commercial television had come to the fore, it had to be geared to that medium. Askit rose to the occasion and came up with what was one of the most successful and longest-running (1971–1994) campaigns ever – The Askit Miseries – which revolved around animated drawings by Roger Hargreaves (creator of the *Mr Men* books) of the ailment characters of headache, cold, flu and sore back. The tagline was 'Askit Fights the Miseries'. Audience reaction was immediately strongly in favour and Askit's image was elevated overnight. The campaign was revolutionary for analgesic advertising. Because visual movement was involved, other media, like bus backs, station signs and hoardings, virtually disappeared, leaving television as the main thrust of any campaign, backed up by press.

The Askit Miseries were replaced by an animated 'Wee Man' in December 1997. The commercials featured the 'Wee Man' cartoon character in humorous situations, one with his head being pounded by a hammer. Askit is then administered for the alleviation of this ailment with the tagline 'Ask for Askit'.

Today the 'Wee Man' is still promoting the benefits of Askit, although he has now become more empowered and is the one administering Askit to people in need. He had become a mirror of the brand – dynamic, active, speedy and powerful.

While today Askit is distributed and marketed in Cumbernauld, the old premises in Saracen Street still stand.

*Information and illustrations courtesy of Askit Laboratories.*

'Wee Man' character from the 'Ask for Askit' campaign which began in December 1997.

# BAXTERS

The Scots are the biggest consumers of soup in Europe, and if there's a company that's famous for the quality of its soups it's Baxters Food Group whose roots go back to 1868.

The beginnings of the world-renowned food manufacturing company were firmly embedded in the Highlands of Scotland and are typical of the success of many Scottish companies still in business today. It was founded by George Baxter, originally one of fifty or so gardeners employed by the Duke of Richmond and Gordon on his estate at Castle Gordon, near Fochabers, on the banks of the River Spey. George then decided that gardening was not for him, and with the backing of his wife, Margaret, the Duke's blessing and a £100 loan from an uncle, he opened a little

George and Margaret Baxter flanking their grocery shop in Spey Street, Fochabers.

grocery shop in Spey Street, Fochabers, in 1868.

With the Scottish virtues of hard work, integrity and initiative behind it, the business prospered. George served in the front of the shop while in the back Margaret made jams and jellies mainly from fruit gathered in the grounds of nearby Castle Gordon. Apart from the locals, their customers included members of shooting and fishing parties and the Duke of Gordon's guests, who, after buying Margaret's jams and jellies and enjoying them, left orders to be delivered to their home addresses.

There was more however to the Baxter shop than groceries and jams. George Baxter was also a whisky wholesaler. He bought malt whisky from local distilleries, bottled it and sold it under the trade name of Baxter's Pure Malt Scotch Whisky. George also travelled to London and Europe for the fine cheeses, pâtés and wines required by the gentry and the Duke of Gordon to whose castle he delivered a daily order which, as well as the imported delicacies, included his wife's jellies and jams.

George Baxter with his son William Alexander Baxter (carrying Gladstone Bag) outside the busy shop in Spey Street, Fochabers.

As he grew up, George and Margaret's son William developed a love for the business, and at thirteen, he left school and joined his father full-time instead of just helping. At an early age, he had shown considerable ability as a salesman and by the time he was eighteen he was accompanying his father on buying visits to London and Europe while his younger brother, George, looked after the shop. His selling trips, however, were not always congenial. His northern route would begin by taking his bicycle by train to Wick

Label from an early product,
Little Scarlet Strawberry Jam.

and then, in all weathers, cycling all the way back to Fochabers, handing out samples and taking orders as he went.

William's wife, Ethel, had a very strong influence on the development of the company for it was she who decided in 1914 that, as sales of jams were so good, she and William should leave the family grocery shop to William's brother, George, and set up on their own as jam manufacturers. To this end, William approached the family's patron, the Duke of Gordon, and after Kirk one Sunday, the Duke and William marked out with wooden pegs and pieces of string a suitable site for a jam factory one mile from Fochabers on the other side of the Spey River. Since then, the factory has been extended many times but is still located on the same beautiful site. The first jam made in the factory was bottled on New Year's morning 1916. While her husband did the travelling, Ethel ran the factory and worked out new recipes.

William ventured beyond the Border in the 1920s. With letters of introduction from the Duke of Gordon, he went to London and obtained orders from such famous companies as Harrod's, Fortnum &

Mason and the Army and Navy Stores. He even received orders from Buckingham Palace. When he gave his sales pitch to the buyer of Fortnum & Mason, however, the buyer said with a smile that he could not understand a word of it. Ethel's preserves, however, spoke for themselves and William still got his order.

In 1929, taking advantage of the ready supply of venison, beef and game in her part of Scotland, the inventive Ethel created and canned the now world-famous Royal Game Soup. She then went on to pioneer soft fruit canning in Scotland and to produce bottled beetroot, canned haggis and more delicious jams and marmalade.

By the end of the 1930s Baxters was known for its quality products, but, in common with other businesses, it was hard hit by the 1939–45 war, and William and Margaret's sons, Gordon and Ian, came back at the end of the war to a depleted workforce of only ten factory workers and one clerk. In 1946 the total turnover was £40,000 and the entire business capital was £4,000.

The rebuilding of the business was put into the hands of Gordon and Ian, and with Gordon covering Scotland as a one-man sales force, as his father had done many years before, and Ian in charge of production, gradually things began to move again despite money being scarce and raw materials being on government allocation. The brothers had to beg for can allocations from the Metal Box Company, and they searched everywhere to source used glass jars for their jams. They were determined to build the business, however, and to base it on

quality products such as Ethel's Royal Game Soup and her beetroot products.

Like Baxter wives before her, Gordon's wife, Ena, an artist, became an important factor in the company's development. She had seen a recipe for a Louisiana chicken gumbo soup in the American magazine *Gourmet* and decided to make it to find out what it was like. However, as it contained an unusual vegetable called okra, a green pepper found in the southern states of America – unobtainable and of course unheard of in Fochabers – she substituted green beans from her garden. The result was a soup about which her husband was so enthusiastic that he wanted to can it immediately. Ena, however, insisted it should be perfected first.

Despite warnings of commercial disaster from well-meaning customers who thought it would be impossible to compete with the giant companies that controlled the British soup market, in 1953 Gordon and Ena introduced a range of Scottish soups and by the third year had sold a million cans. It was an exciting period in the history of the company and the beginning of its post-war growth – 'a Highland romance' as a journalist called it.

Label for Ethel Baxter's famous
Royal Game Soup.

Left. Jam production in the 1960s. Hard work by the look of it.

Right. The ingredients of Baxter's success.

Later came exciting varieties such as Cock-a-leekie, Lobster Bisque, Pheasant Consommé, and Cream of Smoked Trout, all made from local ingredients. Sauces, chutneys, canned game birds and a wide range of traditional Scottish foodstuffs were also produced to Ena's recipes.

Ena Baxter tested all new products in her kitchen at home, and if her family liked them, they were taken to the experimental kitchen at the factory where they were tried out. A cosy family image sold the product, and advertisements showed Ena Baxter chopping and stirring ingredients for soups and sauces to feed her family. The message was that if it was good enough for the Baxter family it was good enough for the Baxter brand.

Baxters exported worldwide and it was rare to see a 'British Week' in international stores without hearing the skirling of Baxter bagpipes in the background. One evening in Chicago, for charity, Gordon and Ena fed 1,250 citizens a Baxter Banquet comprising royal game soup, haggis, pheasants and raspberries. The Banquet helped raise a vast sum for the Scots Old Folks Home in Chicago. As well as Chicago and other American cities, Baxter Banquets and Haggis Parties were given in Australia, Canada,

Denmark, France and Hong Kong. When trying to sell his products in America in the 1950s, Gordon Baxter learned that it is not sufficient to try to sell what you make. You had to first find out what the customer wanted, make it and then advertise it. His discovery changed his business, and he and Ena turned it upside down.

Despite around 182 takeover approaches, the company remains private and is today run by the fourth generation of the Baxter family. Gordon's daughter, Audrey, is the chairman, and she puts the company's continuing success quite simply down to: 'We are passionate at Baxters about good food, which means finding the finest ingredients and creating innovative recipes that are right for today's highly discerning consumers throughout the world.'

Although Baxters has come a long way from its first jams and jellies, it has never lost sight of the natural qualities that made its products so popular initially and, while there is pride in tradition, the company is anything but old-fashioned. It is a highly competitive, sophisticated twenty-first-century business, and the Millennium brought new products such as Noodle Soup in pouches and fresh and frozen soups produced in a new state-of-

the-art factory at Grimsby. Chutneys, sauces for present-day living and meal accompaniments are made at Speyside. Baxters' portfolio of fine products was strengthened by two acquisitions: Garners of Pershore, who produce speciality pickled products, and CCL of Essex, who make a wide variety of high-class salad dressings, mayonnaise, vinaigrettes and sauces.

On a different level, Baxters has become one of Scotland's major tourist attractions. Its Highland Village, overlooking the picturesque River Spey, attracts more than 200,000 visitors each year. The centrepiece is the nineteenth-century Old Museum Shop – a grocery store, complete with long mahogany counter, glass jars, bottles and all the other shopkeeper's paraphernalia of a bygone age. The store, however, is not just a reconstruction of one from the past; it is the original Baxter village shop, which was moved from its site and rebuilt within the Highland Village. There are also two restaurants, a demonstration theatre, a cook-shop and an upmarket speciality shop.

Still a private, very independent family firm, Baxters faces the future with pride and a determination to stay ahead.

*Information and illustrations courtesy of Baxters.*

You could be forgiven for thinking that, in today's world, where children are being conditioned by television, computers, pop music and a love of the latest consumer goods, they would find a comic such as *The Beano*, which is largely unchanged since the 1950s, somewhat dated and boring. You would be wrong, for *The Beano* is the UK's No. 1 comic,

Lord Snooty, or Lord Marmaduke of Bunkerton, to give him his full title.

with a weekly circulation of over 120,000. Children love its propaganda-free timeless humour, stemming from the activities of naughty characters such as Dennis the Menace, Minnie the Minx, Roger the Dodger and the Bash Street Kids, who flout authority and cause mayhem in domestic situations, at school and in all other areas of life.

Following on the success of *The Dandy*, introduced on 4 December 1937, Dundee publisher D. C. Thomson launched a sister comic, *The Beano*, on 30 July 1938. It cost 2d (less than 1p) at which price it remained until 1960. Very few copies of the early *Beanos* exist, and a copy of *Beano* No. 1 was sold for £12,000 in 2004, a record for a British comic that will probably be surpassed. Not a bad return for 2d.

*The Dandy* and *Beano* created fantasy worlds in which children could question the probability of their exploits but not the standards of their behaviour or attitudes. There was a moral code. Parental and school authority might be challenged, but there was inevitably a punishment to suit the crime. The humour was basic, the fun stemming

from a wide selection of cartoon characters whom readers could relate to, sympathise with and laugh at in ridiculous incidents and situations, set against the social conditions of the time. Pure slapstick was avoided.

Today the comics' editors are ever conscious of the unique hold their characters have on their readers, and while the humour is unchanged, with maturity came responsibility – such as when the Home Office asked that care be taken when using fireworks in stories. Now November 5 is not marked at all. Corporal punishment was banned, not because of any concern that psychologists expressed on the so-called violence of comic strips but because the editors agreed that the social conditions of the time must be reflected.

The first cartoon character to appear on the cover of *The Beano* was Big Eggo, the ostrich who would eat anything in sight, from anvils to Second World War bombs. His first words were: 'Someone's taken my egg again.' Eggo remained on the cover until 1948 when Biffo the Bear

*The Beano*'s first cover, introducing Big Eggo, the ostrich who ate everything in sight.

The format of *The Beano* was similar to that of *The Dandy*: twenty-eight pages with a mix of short, funny strips, adventure picture stories and text stories. Among the adventure stories was the tiniest character in comic history, Tom Thumb. There was also the Shipwrecked Circus and Jimmy and His Magic Patch. Jimmy Watson had a patch made from a piece of magic carpet sewn on to the seat of his trousers and, by simply wishing out loud, he was whisked back in time to have adventures with historical and legendary characters such as Sinbad the Sailor, William Tell and Ali Baba. All these stories were drawn by Dudley Dexter Watkins whose genius created some of the finest cartoon characters in history and to whom much of the early success of *The Dandy* and *Beano* can be attributed.

One of Dudley Watkins' most famous characters was the cow-pie-eating hero Desperate Dan, who first appeared in *The Dandy* in 1937 and was said to be modelled on Albert Barnes, the then editor of *The Dandy*. Dudley was also responsible for giving us Oor Wullie and The Broons and was the only cartoonist at D. C. Thomson who was allowed to sign his work.

Soon after the launch of *The Beano* came the Second World War, and, although shortage of paper meant that *The Beano* and *The Dandy* were reduced to twelve pages per issue and publication fortnightly (on alternate weeks), it was felt that to continue publishing the comics would help keep up the morale of the nation's children. Although the comics were non-political in peacetime, the war years saw an element of propaganda in

took over. Free inside the first issue was a Whoopee Mask, only one of which is known still to exist. Also in the first issue was Lord Snooty, or Lord Marmaduke of Bunkerton, to give him his full title. Snooty, clad in a top hat, Eton collar, bow tie, waistcoat, bum-freezer jacket and striped trousers, had to sneak out of his castle to play with the local kids as it was not 'done' for someone of his class to mix with 'commoners'. His guardian, Aunt Matilda, however, took pity on him and invited his common pals to the castle. Lord Snooty was dropped in 1988 because children could no longer identify with him.

Biffo the Bear who went straight to the front cover when introduced on 24 January 1948.

Dennis the Menace and (below) his dog Gnasher.

Roger The Dodger, whose ingenuity in dodging work knew no bounds.

support of the British war effort. Two liquorice black eyes were given as a gift in 1940. This was to be the last gift for over twenty years.

Publication restrictions continued after the war, and by 1947 the comics were down to ten pages, which was increased to twelve in 1948 at which figure they remained until 1960 when they were increased to sixteen pages. In 1971, they went up to twenty pages. Weekly publication was resumed in 1949 and a year later the word 'comic' was dropped from the titles.

When Biffo the Bear was introduced on 24 January 1948, he went straight to the front cover. While in the early years, his stories were told in pictures without any speech balloons, eventually words were put into his mouth and he lasted until 1986 when he was rested. When he returned in 1989 he had lost his voice again. A mystery remains. Why does he have a human aunt?

When the wartime restrictions were finally over, the comics gradually returned to normal, with *The Dandy* narrowly the top seller. Then ... kaboom! ... on 17 March 1951, Dennis the Menace, drawn by David Law, exploded on to the pages of *The Beano*. Dennis was the first of a stream of gently anarchic revolutionaries, 'loveable rogues' who broke the mould of the fantasy-based characters that had populated *The Beano* until then.

On his first appearance, Dennis was labelled as 'the wildest boy in the world', and for the first few episodes he did not wear his famous red and black hooped jersey – his mum was still knitting it. Dennis's first words were: 'keep off the grass. huh!' In 1968, Dennis's faithful sidekick,

Gnasher, an extremely rare Abyssinian wire-haired tripe hound, joined in the mayhem. Gnasher was modelled on Dennis's black hair, to which were added eyes, nose, legs, and teeth that could bite through granite. Dennis made the cover in 1974, and two years later the Dennis the Menace Fan Club (including Gnasher's Fang Club) was formed. As well as having Gnasher as a pet, in 1979 Dennis acquired Rasher the Pig. There was a Gnational emergency in 1986, when Gnasher went missing for eight weeks. When he returned he had six menacing pups with him – Gnatasha, Gnaomi, Gnanette, Gnorah, Gnancy and Gnaughty Gnipper, his son and heir.

The second of the new breed of characters was Roger the Dodger, who began ducking, dodging and diving on 18 April 1953. Drawn by Ken Reid, Roger earned his title, 'the craftiest schoolboy on earth', by using his endless collection of 'dodge' books to avoid doing any work. His ingenuity in dodging work knew no

Minnie the Minx, the female counterpart of Dennis the Menace, Minnie's hero.

bounds. In fact, he would have dodged breathing if he could have got someone else to do it for him! Roger's first words in *The Beano* were: 'I'm going out before dad makes me do my homework!'

After Roger came Minnie the Minx, who has made life a misery for her mum and dad and anyone else who has dared to cross her path since she appeared on 19 December 1953 with the words: 'Yes, ma dear!' (quickly followed by) 'Oo-woo-woo! I'm on the warpath! take that, Charlie!' Dressed like her male counterpart and hero, Dennis the Menace, in a red and black hooped jersey, her famous red pompomed beret, which doubles as a deadly Frisbee, hid her red hair, proving that red means danger. Minnie specialised in obliterating little boys by the dozen, with sweeping punches. She was, if anything, more devastating to her surroundings than Dennis. Minnie was the work of artist Leo Baxendale.

The last of the revolutionaries was a gang whose members arrived on 13 February 1954. The strip, consisting of three introductory pictures and one large frame of a chaotic scene, began as 'When the Bell Rings' with the words: 'Hi, sleepy! Open the door — it's four.' Two years later, the gang became the Bash Street Kids, who struck terror into the heart of their teacher. Although the Bash Street Kids usually get the better of their teacher, they don't beat him up, nor do they vandalise the classroom and in the end authority usually asserts itself. The terrors of class IIb are Danny, Toots, Plug, Fatty, Wilfrid, 'Erbert, Sidney, Spotty and Smiffy.

The idea for the Bash Street Kids came to *The Beano*'s first editor, George Moonie, as he looked out of his window, which faced the playground of Dundee's High School. As he watched the children play there was mayhem, and he realised that this was what he wanted for a strip. George commissioned Leo Baxendale to draw it, and *The Beano*'s readership so loved the antics of the nine rascals who became the Bash Street Kids that by 1962 only Dennis the Menace was more popular.

Episodes of the Bash Street Kids no longer end with the teacher setting about the children with his cane. Punishments such as clamping their skateboards are used instead, and although the Kids are still dressed as 1950s' children in shorts, jumpers, caps and lace-up shoes rather than jeans and trainers, they now have mobile phones and play computer games. Their speech has also been updated. They used to speak the Queen's English with proper grammar, the only slang being the occasional 'Cripes'. Now they use Americanised slang such as

The Bash Street Kids.

Ivy the Terrible whose ambition is to be the 'toughest kid in *The Beano!*'

the sarcastic 'Not!' They will also say things like 'Lemme outta here!' There was a national outcry when the Kids were made politically correct in 1993 when a spoof episode put them in a hi-tech school and made them well behaved. Readers did not want them well behaved — they loved their rebellious antics.

The success of the newcomers, who attracted a huge following among young readers who could only dream of matching the exploits of the young revolutionaries, gradually led to a change of content for *The Beano*. When, by asking readers for their views, it was discovered that the funny comic strips were by far the most popular items, first the text stories disappeared, then the adventure stories.

Over the decades other new characters, like Billy Whizz, the only boy to have run around the world and zoomed through so many time zones that he got back two days before he left, joined the terrible four of Dennis, Roger, Minnie and the Bash Street Kids. So did Ivy the Terrible, a junior recruit whose tantrums measure at the higher end of the Richter Scale. She erupted in the comic with the words: 'Hi, readers, I'm Ivy, and I'm going to be

the toughest kid in *The Beano!*' Calamity James, the world's unluckiest boy, made his first ill-fated appearance in 1985.

Bea, Dennis the Menace's baby sister, arrived in 1998. Her proper name was Beatrice, but she was quickly renamed Bea because of her striking yellow and black hooped romper suit. It was soon clear that she had much in common with her big brother. Robbie Rebel arrived in January 2002 with one word — no!!

While the heart of *The Beano* is still rooted in the stars introduced in the 1950s, the characters remain fresh by reacting to the modern world — Roger the Dodger can store his best dodges on a hard disk and the most enduring character, Dennis the Menace, has traded his cartie for a futuristic, gadget-filled Menace car. Dennis and Co. can also be found in jigsaws, as figurines, on spectacles, motorcycle helmets and cake-mix packs, to name but a few. In 1996, Dennis and Gnasher became TV stars in an animated series on BBC.

In 1998, *The Beano* Club was launched, signing up 50,000 members in its first year. Every member, including personality honorary members like Sean Connery, Princes Harry and William, Stephen Hendry and Michael Owen, received their T-shirt, poster, practical jokes and other goodies plus regular deliveries of newsletters and birthday cards.

In April 2000, the Beanoland fun-zone of Chessington World of Adventures was opened, offering kids the chance to experience attractions such as Billy's Whizzer, Roger's Dodgems and Dennis's Madhouse.

At the 2002 British Comic

Awards, *The Beano* was voted Best Comic Now, Best Comic Ever. Gnasher received the Best Supporting Character Award.

In *The Beano*'s 65th birthday edition, all the characters were up to their usual tricks, especially Dennis the Menace who did his best to cause mayhem at the birthday celebrations. He was allowed into the party, however, when he signed a promise of good behaviour: 'I promise not to throw jelly at Softy Walter, make rude noises, bite table legs . . .'

Many characters have come and gone in *The Beano*'s lifetime. Most traits, habits, attributes and characteristics have been exploited and are still being exploited — nosiness, greed, cowardice, absent-mindedness, mischief-making, sneakiness, courage, strength and exceptional skills. When characters no longer appeal, updated ones take their place.

That the old-age pensioner *Beano*, with its style largely unchanged since the 1950s, is Britain's favourite comic proves that children still love good old-fashioned knockabout fun, especially when it knocks authority. The comic has never lost touch with its readers and will surely continue to delight generations to come with fun-loving characters that will embrace new trends and technology as the years go by.

Robbie Rebel

The cover of *The Beano*'s 65th birthday edition shows, as well as Dennis the Menace, characters from the past such as Big Eggo, Tin Can Tommy, Pin the Elastic Man, Tom Thumb, Big Fat Joe, Whoopee Hank and Morgan the Mighty.

# BROWN & POLSON CORNFLOUR

Cornflour, used by cooks worldwide to thicken soups, sauces and gravies, was first produced in Paisley by Brown & Polson. The history of the company began in 1840 when two muslin manufacturers, William Brown & Son and John Polson & Co., formed a joint enterprise to find a starch to bleach the muslin they produced. (The firm of William Brown had recently located to Paisley from Glasgow.) The joint enterprise, comprising a partner from each firm, John Polson Snr and William Brown, set up a bleaching, scouring and starching works at Thrushcraigs, near Paisley.

While researching for the most suitable starch for the two companies' finished muslin goods, John Polson discovered that a mixture of sago and flour made an ideal starch that could withstand bleaching. The idea then occurred to him that the starch might be suitable for household use, and in 1842 he introduced 'Powder Starch', which was first sold in Edinburgh in packages at a penny and upwards. The name 'Powder Starch' came about as, for the first time, the starch was not in the form of 'pipes' or 'crystals' resembling basaltic column in miniature, the only form in which it had previously been known. Because it was the only starch available to the domestic market, Powder Starch was a huge success

Early Packaging for
Brown & Polson's Patent Corn Flour

and was awarded a certificate of merit at the Great Exhibition of 1851.

John Polson Senior died in 1843, at the early age of forty-three, just a year after the introduction of Powder Starch. After his death, the firms of William Brown & Son and John Polson & Co. were amalgamated as Brown & Polson (Royal Starch Works).

The greatest breakthrough in the history of Brown & Polson came from John Polson Jnr, who discovered that if the fatty content was extracted from maize (also known as Indian corn) the substance remaining was a palatable pure starch. John then took out a patent in 1854 to market it as a foodstuff and soon the first packets of 'Brown & Polson's Patent Corn Flour' were in the shops. The new product, used as a basis for blancmanges, custards, baby and invalid foods, and as a thickener for soups and gravies, made the company world famous. Later the name was changed to 'cornflour' without capital letters.

As the firm prospered, new buildings were required and the original works at Thrushcraigs were supplemented by others at Barterholm and Colinslee. Eventually all these were concentrated at Carriagehill, Paisley, and then at splendid new works in the town's Falside Road. These new works were described in 1881, in a 'Treatise on the manufacture of Starch, etc.' by Robert Hutter of Philadelphia, as among 'the most gigantic establishments of the kind'. The business continued to grow, and by 1896 it was described thus: 'Suppose that all the bags of Indian corn crushed at these works in one year were piled on top of each other, they would form a column 80 miles high.' In Paisley, Brown & Polson workers were always recognisable as they were usually covered in a white coating of flour.

John Polson was deeply concerned about the welfare of his workers, and in the 1870s he introduced a profit-sharing scheme in the form of a yearly bonus based on the firm's profits. The bonus was paid to workers provided they were not 'guilty of misdemeanour', and to teach them a lesson in thrift, the bonus was paid directly to their credit in the local savings bank.

By the turn of the century Brown & Polson had become the largest manufacturer of starch products in Britain. Its best-known products were Patent Cornflour, Paisley Flour, Raisley Flour (self-raising), Blancmange, and Custard Powder. Later the company produced Mazola cooking oil as a by-product of maize. (It is interesting to note that over the years the by-products of maize were incorporated into the making of not only margarine and paper but into the life-saving medicines of streptomycin and penicillin.)

Advertisement 1934 for Zesto Corn Flakes made in Paisley by Brown & Polson.

Following the death of John Polson in 1900, the business was continued by J. Armour Brown and his three sons who were later joined by Lord Rowallan, connected by marriage to the Polson family.

Although by the start of the 1930s Brown & Polson was still the largest starch manufacturing company in the UK, the plant was old and new capital was required. To this end, in 1935 Brown & Polson became a wholly owned subsidiary of Corn Products Company Ltd, an affiliate company of the American Corn Products Refining Company which had a manufacturing site in Manchester.

Throughout the years, the original firm published cookery books promoting the use of cornflour and custard powder. One was called *Light Fare Recipes for Corn Flour and 'Raisley' Cookery*, and as well as containing recipes for culinary delights such as 'Paisley Rolls' and

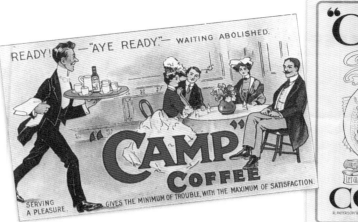

Ready Aye Ready – waiting abolished. Postcard c.1905 that plays on the product's instant readiness for use whenever wanted, with no loss of time waiting until beans were ground.

Camp advertisement, 1909, cleverly adapted from Glasgow's famous coat of arms. St Mungo is shown enjoying a steaming cup of Camp Coffee.

depicts an Indian sepoy serving a cup of Camp to a kilted British officer outside his tent in some far outpost of the Empire. It is thought that the model for the officer was Sir Hector MacDonald, a general in the Boer War. Only his head was used, however. The uniform was deliberately drawn to avoid representing that of any particular regiment. It was also thought that to show a general might provoke ill-feeling and possibly action by the War Office. In 1954, when the company tried to register the 'Highlander' alone as a trademark, the War Office would not allow a soldier in uniform to be used in such a way. A few years later, the registration was accepted. The motto on the label – 'Ready Aye Ready' – is not traceable to any particular family but was used as a battle cry by several clans.

By 1898, Paterson was exporting coffee essence to all Britain's dependencies, and as every soldier in Queen Victoria's army throughout the Empire had a bottle of Camp tucked away in his kitbag, it was just as likely to be drunk around a campfire in the Khyber Pass as in a Glasgow drawing room. The Canadian, Australian and New Zealand markets were especially strong, but stringent tariffs according to value on both essence and bottles kept Paterson's from expanding into the lucrative American market.

While the prominent position of Camp was undoubtedly due to the excellence of the product, it was backed up by some of the most effective advertising of the day, earning Paterson's product international acclaim and recognition. Advertisements were always eye-catching and, regardless of the form – poster, show card or general press – were highly creative and artistic. The colonial image was fully exploited at trade fairs and exhibitions, and displays included full-scale castellated fortresses made from Camp Coffee cases and bivouacs shaped as caves inside which people tasted the coffee.

Paterson was the leading coffee essence producer in the Empire, and although there were well over one hundred producers of coffee essence or extract in Britain, the sales of Camp equalled the total sales of *all* the other producers.

In 1909, Campbell Paterson and his two sons, Robert and James, formed a private limited company and made coffee essence its sole business. Campbell Paterson died in the Channel Islands in 1920.

Camp Coffee's popularity was confirmed in both world wars when sales were sacrificed to maintain quality while coffee was scarce. It is remarkable that, despite the success of instant coffee, output of Camp trebled between 1939 and the early 1950s, by which time the company had become a public one.

Today Camp Coffee essence is produced by McCormick Foods, but not in Scotland.

Show card of 1935 with a military theme, as had the company's early advertisements.

# COATS

The story of Coats, the world leader in thread, began with James Coats, the son of George Coats who, around 1760, moved from Dykehead to Paisley where he took up weaving. He married Catherine Heywood in 1763, and their son James was born in 1774. James was destined to become a weaver but after completing an apprenticeship, at the age of sixteen, he joined the Ayrshire Fencibles, serving for six years in the south of England. When he was discharged, he walked from London to Paisley, having been given just 2s. 6d. (12.5p) when he left the army.

Back in Paisley, James set up in business as a weaver and in 1802 married Katherine Mitchell, who employed a number of girls tambouring (embroidering) cloth. When ill health forced James to give up weaving, he joined his wife in her trade. He then began manufacturing Canton crepe shawls, which were fashionable at the time. He had bought one for his wife in London and decided to try to make them as no one in Scotland did so. The crepe material was made of silk and, as the process required special knowledge

and skill, James's first attempts failed. However, when he found that his friend, weaver James Whyte, was also trying to produce the same type of shawl, they went into partnership and mastered the process successfully.

James's entry into manufacturing thread came about through his association with Ross and Duncan, the company that produced the special twisted silk thread required for his shawls. He had become a silent partner in this firm, and as his contract was due to end in 1826, he built his own thread mill in Ferguslie, Paisley, in 1824. He had seen the possibilities for cotton sewing thread and realised that the method of producing it was not much different from that used in producing his shawl yarn. The investment was made despite a slump in the textile trade, with over 1,000 weavers becoming unemployed.

When James retired in 1830, he left the weaving business to his partners and to his son William. His thread business was taken over by his sons James and Peter, who rented the mill from their father for

£500 per annum and formed the partnership of J & P Coats. James and Peter's brother Thomas joined the partnership shortly after the firm was set up.

By 1839, the business had prospered and expanded, and as 75 per cent of the thread it produced was exported to the United States, another brother, Andrew, went there to manage sales. Once in the States, he found that Coats' thread was being sold under their American customers' own names instead of the Coats' label. Realising the weaknesses of Coats' selling arrangements, Andrew felt it would be practical to establish the American trade in its own name. On proposing this to Paisley, however, there were doubts as it was feared that its American customers would transfer their orders to other manufacturers. Nevertheless, by the end of 1840, J & P Coats sent the first shipment of threads to America for sale under its own name.

The 1840s ended with Coats' thread being the leader in the American market, despite other firms' attempts to topple it. Sales were to get even better, however,

This illustration of girls at work in J & P Coats' Ferguslie thread mill shows how vast the establishment was.

for in Boston in 1851 Isaac Singer marketed the first domestic sewing machine for which Coats manufactured the strong, but fine, cotton thread it required.

Such was the reputation of Coats' thread in America that forgeries were common, with some manufacturers producing three-cord thread of 150 yards and labelling it as J & P Coats' best six-cord thread or some offshoot of the Coats'

name. (Coats' threads were all six cord and 200 yards long.) Andrew Coats raised many court actions, and in one day alone took sixteen of the largest wholesale dealers in New York to court, one of which sold 130,000 dozen spools.

By 1860 Paisley was the most important centre of cotton thread manufacturing in the world, with around a dozen companies involved. Two of these were the largest in the world, J & P Coats and J & J Clark of Seedhill Mills (later Anchor Mills), the leader in the home market, which had begun in 1812.

The agreeable trading situation in the United States ended when the Americans imposed a high import duty on finished thread. They had decided that foreigners should no longer supply them with material for making up their garments. To preserve the trade already built up, therefore, Coats had no option

The message in Coats' advertisement was that the company's thread was reliable and strong. For the sake of the cats in this charming advertisment, let's hope so.

other than to manufacture in the United States, and in 1870 thread mills at Pawtucket, Rhode Island, were built that grew to be as large as the Ferguslie mills.

With the transfer of the Ferguslie production for the US market to Pawtucket, there was an urgent need for expansion in the British, European and other markets so that the Ferguslie mills' production capacity could be maximised. To this end, Archibald Coats (Peter Coats' son and by the 1870s in charge at Ferguslie under Thomas Coats' general control) managed to increase sales in the home market by concentrating on a few high-quality products such as Coats' standard 200-yard black-and-white six-cord spools for the household trade, together with some other lengths and colours. These were sold increasingly under the company's 'Chain' trademark.

Archibald Coats, however, had little knowledge of foreign markets and relied on the existing system of agencies, which he extended. Although sales increased greatly, he grew increasingly dissatisfied with the selling system in foreign markets. Consequently, in 1878, he created a new position at Ferguslie – foreign sales manager – to which he appointed Otto Ernst Philippi from the company's Hamburg agency. Born in Germany, Philippi had become a British citizen in 1872, and Archibald had been attracted to his flow of ideas, his command of languages and – it is said – the fineness of his writing.

Philippi's first assignment was to go to Central and South America to explore possibilities, establish agents systematically, and generally lay the foundations for increased exports to

Coats' main competitor, Clark & Co.'s Anchor Mill in Paisley.

these areas. This successfully completed, Philippi was given responsibility for promoting sales in foreign markets except in the United States. (He later became overall sales director.)

The effects of Philippi's appointment were rapid, and he became the focus of dynamic growth in the firm. In 1889, he introduced a joint selling agreement with Coats' main competitor, Clark & Co. This made sense, as competition was fierce, with both companies selling the same articles in the same limited markets worldwide and making narrow profit margins. The agreement, the Sewing Cotton Agency, was formalised a year later as the Central Agency and, as well as Coats and Clark, it included Brook Brothers of Meltham, Yorkshire, a smaller but effective competitor.

The year 1889 was also when Philippi took Coats into production in Russia as the major partner in a joint venture with Clark and Brook.

This was because of the establishment of a formidable Russian competitor and to avoid the possibility of increased Russian import duties.

Coats became a limited liability company in 1890 with a capital of £5.75 million. While the flotation strengthened the company, competition remained strong worldwide, and in May 1896 Coats and Clark amalgamated, together with Brook Brothers and Chadwick of Eagley Mills, Bolton. The new company took the name of the largest and wealthiest member – J & P Coats – but each arm maintained its own identity, preserving the names and trademarks used for the particular markets or qualities with which they were associated. The merger made J & P Coats the largest thread combine in the world.

The period from the amalgamation to the death of chairman Archibald Coats in 1912 was one of stable growth as world population, real income and demand for clothing and household goods rose, and by 1913 Coats had mills in Russia, Austria, Spain, Belgium, Poland, Hungary, Germany, Italy, Portugal, Switzerland, Brazil, Mexico and Japan. Selling was through the Central Agency network.

During the First World War two of the Ferguslie mills produced khaki thread and Egyptian cotton thread for the production of aircraft wings. Mill workers received war bonuses depending on their peacetime wages.

The Second World War again brought the production of khaki thread, and the company paid an allowance to any of their male workers who joined the armed services. With the men joining up, women became drivers, tenters, etc., and some were seconded to other reserve industries. Overtime was prominent, and tea with two buns was supplied during the half-hour tea break.

While an effect of the Second World War was the loss of mills in Russia and East European countries such as Poland, Hungary, Romania and Czechoslovakia, after 1945 new units were established in places such as India, Venezuela and Hong Kong.

The 1960s began with diversification, which, along with trading difficulties in the UK, the emergence of cheap textile products and cheaper labour costs in other countries, contributed to the decline and eventually the demise of thread production in Paisley. Until then, Coats had mainly concentrated in making thread in the UK and abroad. In 1961, however, the merger of Coats with Paton & Baldwin, creating the Coats Paton Group, brought about extensive expansion into the clothing industry with the acquisition of companies such as Jaeger and Pasolds, and producers of children's wear including the Ladybird brand. Country Casuals, a chain of women's fashion shops was opened in 1973. With the merger in 1986 of Coats Paton with Vantona Viyella, creating Coats Viyella, products such as carpets and home furnishings (the Dorma brand) were acquired. There were also numerous acquisitions of a non-textile nature.

Diversification continued to do the company no favours, and in

Advertisement of 1967 for Coats' thread. The theme of this advertisement echoes those of the early days – the reliability and strength of the thread.

1981 the Ferguslie Mill closed along with half of the Anchor Mill, which shut for good in 1993, ending an association with Paisley that had lasted for 181 years.

In 1991 the acquisition of Tootal extended Coats' global thread cover, notably in key Asian markets. Another foray into thread-making was made in 1999 with the acquisition of Barbour, the world market leader in specialty thread.

The twenty-first century started with Coats withdrawing from much of its non-threadmaking businesses to concentrate of what it always did best, manufacturing and selling thread, a strategy that allows the company to face the future with confidence.

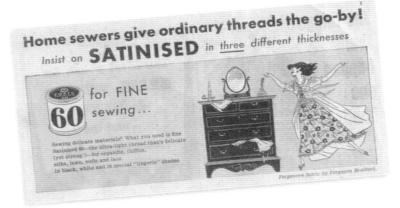

Advertisement of 1952 for Coats Satinised Thread.

Information and illustrations courtesy of Coats.

John Dewar

Tommy Dewar

Glass bottle that John Dewar used for his blends instead of kegs or stone jars as was the custom.

John Dewar & Sons produce the biggest selling Scotch whisky in the US, and its Dewar's 12 is the fastest growing deluxe whisky in the world.

Dewar's origins go back to John Dewar, born in 1805 in the small village of Dull, near Aberfeldy. After leaving school he was apprenticed to a joiner, after which he joined his relative Alex MacDonald's wine and spirits business in Perth as a cellarman. Although he became a partner in his relative's business in 1837, in 1846 he decided to start his own business, and in a little shop at 111 High Street, Perth, he set up as a wine and spirit merchant. The business flourished, and as whisky became its dominant aspect, he began blending his own from several different producers to give it a mellower flavour.

At first Dewar sold in and around Perth, but gradually during the 1860s he extended his area by employing a traveller to go further afield for orders. It is said

111 High Street, Perth

Aberfeldy Distillery in 1899. It was built in 1898 to ensure a plentiful supply of malt whisky for blending purposes.

that he was the first person to start selling his blends in glass bottles, which were labelled with the name of his brand, instead of using a keg or plain stone jars as was the custom at the time.

In 1871, one of Dewar's ten children, John Alexander, joined the business, and in 1879, at the age of 23, he became a partner. A year later John Dewar senior died and John, a skilled whisky blender as well as a talented businessman, took over the firm.

Round about 1884, John's brother, 20-year-old Thomas, known as Tommy, joined the firm, having been trained in Leith and Glasgow with Robertson & Baxter, the well-known firm of wine and spirit merchants. When Tommy became a partner a few years later, he persuaded his brother to go for the English market, where whisky had traditionally sold poorly next to spirits like brandy, rum and gin.

Having a knack for marketing, Tommy set off for London in 1885 with introductions to only two men, one of whom he discovered was dead and the other bankrupt. Despite this setback, through hard

work and determination Tommy managed to create a demand for Dewar's whisky, which had won a medal at the Edinburgh Exhibition in 1886.

In 1890 Tommy secured an exclusive contract to supply Scotch whisky to top catering firm Spiers and Pond, whose customers included railway buffets, hotels and music venues. It was said that Tommy was probably more responsible than anyone else for the success of Scotch whisky in London.

During the 1890s, Tommy took a stand at the Brewers' Exhibition in Birmingham, where he was given a small remote stand hidden from the crowds. His way of being noticed was to hire a kilt-wearing Highland piper to stand beside the Dewar's exhibit, playing at full blast and drowning out all other sound. Naturally the other exhibitors complained, but Tommy, having previously checked that music was permitted, refused to stop his piper playing, thus ensuring significant newspaper coverage.

Dewar's business flourished, and in order to ensure supplies of whisky, the firm leased the Tullymet

distillery in Ballinluig, south-east of Pitlochry, from the Duke of Atholl. It also purchased a bonded warehouse at Speygate in Perth.

1891 brought some unanticipated free publicity in the United States. Dunfermline-born American millionaire Andrew Carnegie had written to John Dewar & Sons asking for a small keg of Dewar's whisky to be shipped to President Benjamin Harrison, the bill to be sent to Carnegie. The president, however, was blasted in the press for supporting a foreign brand and not domestic bourbon. While not good publicity for the president, it was for Dewar's, as its name appeared in newspapers around the States. Enquiries and orders for the firm's whisky rolled in, and a quote from Tommy at the time reads, 'It was the very best advertisement I ever had, and certainly the cheapest.'

In 1892 Tommy began a two-year sales trip, when he visited 26 countries, appointed 32 agents and arranged for opening consignments to each country he had visited. The Dewar brand was put on the map worldwide. Out of press articles and reports which were based on the

speeches Tommy gave at industry and political gatherings came pithy sayings known as Dewarisms, a few samples of which are found below.
—If you think you know it all, you are missing something.
—We should not say how is business, but where is business.
—Never invest in a going concern until you know which way it is going.

Tommy kept a journal of his travels, and in 1904 it was published, entitled *A Ramble Round The Globe.* The book was a medley of social observations and whimsical anecdotes.

In 1893 the firm received Queen Victoria's Royal Warrant, and around 1895 an office was opened in Bleecker Street in New York. On a personal front, in 1895 Tommy became the third person in Britain to buy a car, the other two being the Prince of Wales and Thomas Lipton. Tommy's car was a 3½ hp chain-driven Benz, and its highest running cost was for teams of horses to tow it home.

To ensure a plentiful supply of malt whisky for blending purposes for its expanding empire, in 1898 Dewar's built a new distillery at Aberfeldy. Also in 1898, Tommy commissioned the first ever motion picture advertisement for a beverage. Produced by the Edison Company, the film of a dancing Scotsman was projected on to the roof of a building in New York's Herald Square, causing traffic to stop.

In 1899, what was to become Dewar's most popular blend, White Label, was introduced. It had been created by the firm's first appointed Master Blender, A. J. Cameron. From then on, only the Master Blender could unlock the secrets of this closely guarded recipe.

Before 1908, when the firm's new office, Dewar House in London's Haymarket, was being built,

The famous White Label marching drum major advertisement of 1953 that became known worldwide.

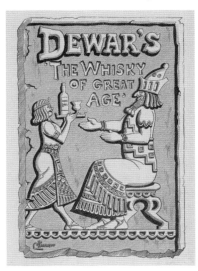

An advertisement c1903 on 'The Whisky of Great Age' Egyptian theme.

Advertisement c1930s entitled 'The Spirit of Give and Take'. The illustration was the work of Geoffrey Squire, who painted many of Dewar's advertisements at the time.

Tommy had acquired, as an interim head office and bottling centre, Dewar's Wharf, on the south bank of the Thames near Waterloo Bridge. The site included the 200 feet-high Shot Tower, and about 1910/1911 the firm erected on it the largest mechanical sign in Europe. It showed a 68-foot-tall Highlander 'drawn' with coloured electric light bulbs. The action of the programmed electric circuit made the Highlander pour out and drink glasses of Dewar's whisky while his beard and kilt fluttered in the wind. Above the Highlander's bonnet, the name DEWAR blazed out, dominating the landscape.

In 1915 John Dewar & Sons merged with the large whisky blending firm of James Buchanan to form a holding company, Scotch Whisky Brands Ltd, that in 1919 was renamed Buchanan-Dewar. In 1923, to ensure supplies of whisky for blending, the company bought distilleries at Ord, Parkmore, Pulteney and Aultmore.

In 1925, along with John Walker & Sons Ltd, Buchanan-Dewar merged with the Distillers Company Ltd (DCL), created in 1877 by a merger of six distillers. John and Tommy Dewar joined the board of DCL.

Keeping up its reputation for innovative advertising, in 1927, Dewar produced the first documentary on the production and blending of whisky. Filmed at Aberfeldy Distillery and the company's office in Perth, it documented the entire process, from the ingredients through to distilling, blending, bottling and despatch.

John Dewar died in November 1929 and Tommy in April 1930. The brothers had performed different roles within the company. John in Perth had looked after administration and production, while Tommy, whose charisma was a large asset to the brand, travelled the world promoting it. John had married and had remained in his native Perthshire, where he lived in Dupplin Castle. Tommy had not married and had lived in his estate of Homestall in Sussex, where he bred dogs and racehorses.

On a public front, in 1900 the Dewar brothers had been elected to Parliament, Tommy representing the Conservatives and John the Liberals. Tommy received a knighthood in 1901 and John a baronetcy in 1907. In 1917 John had become Baron Forteviot of Dupplin, the first of the 'Whisky Barons'. In 1919 Tommy became Baron Dewar of Homestall. It was not purely for

their services to the whisky industry that the brothers were honoured, for each had served their cities with distinction by holding a variety of public offices.

After the death of the brothers, their work was carried on by Peter Dewar, not a relative, who was chairman of the company from 1930 to 1946. It was he who saw it through the difficult days of the Second World War, when in 1939 the government ordered distilleries to produce only one third of their previous year's production to conserve barley. The company was

Aberfeldy Distillery at the present day

forced to lay off its sales force as it rationed orders at home and abroad and production at Aberfeldy Distillery halted from 1942 to 1944. During World War I the distillery had been closed from 1917 to 1919.

In 1953 came one of the company's most important events, when Monty Girling, a Gordon Highlander, posed in full Highland dress for a photographer while stationed in Aberdeen. The picture became the basis for Dewar's famous 'marching drum major' logo, one of the world's best-known commercial images. A statue of the Highlander stands in the grounds of Aberfeldy Distillers.

Between 1966 and 1984, John

Dewar & Sons won six Queen's awards for Export Achievement, and during the 1960s began the rebuilding of its Aberfeldy Distillery that was completed in 1972.

Between 1960 and 1980, Dewar's sales expanded both at home and abroad, and by 1980 Dewar's White Label had become the top-selling whisky in the United States. In 1986, Guinness acquired the Distillers Company and John Dewar & Sons in a hostile takeover. In 1998 Bacardi bought Dewar's, amalgamating it with its other whisky brand, William Lawson's. As part of the deal Bacardi also purchased four distilleries – Aultmore, Craigellachie, Aberfeldy and Royal Brackla.

The year 2000 was an important one for Dewar's. It introduced its premium product, Dewar's 12-year-old Scotch Whisky blend, now the fastest growing deluxe whisky in the world. It also opened Dewar's World of Whisky, a £2 million visitor's centre, at the Aberfeldy distillery.

More than a century and a half after its founder began blending whisky in Perth, Dewar continues to produce fine distilled beverages, and today the company owns five distilleries – Aberfeldy, Craigellachie, Royal Brackla, Aultmore and Macduff. All produce whisky for Dewar's blends, as well as limited-edition malt scotches. Dewar's expanded portfolio includes Dewar's 18-Year-Old, Dewar's Signature, and Aberfeldy 12-Year-Old and 21-Year-Old single malt whiskies. Recent investments include a £120 million project to build new blending and warehousing facilities in Glasgow.

Information and illustrations courtesy Dewar & Sons

# DRAMBUIE

Mist-shrouded isles, heather-covered hills, a handsome prince, loyal followers, mystery, murder and intrigue! A synopsis for a film script or a novel? No, it's that of a true story – the incredible ancestry of Drambuie, the only British liqueur to be exported to every major world market.

Drambuie, a combination of whiskies blended with herbal essence and heather honey, owes its origins to Prince Charles Edward Stuart and Captain John MacKinnon, a native of Skye and a fervent supporter of the Jacobite cause.

With the defeat at Culloden in 1746, all the Prince's aspirations of gaining a crown vanished. His small army of poorly equipped Highlanders stood no chance against the Duke of Cumberland's forces. After the battle, no mercy was shown to the Jacobites, and the Duke more than earned his title of 'Butcher Cumberland'.

Although Charles had a price on his head of £30,000, no one betrayed him, and for five months a small band of friends sheltered him until he was smuggled aboard a ship for France, never to return to Scotland. John MacKinnon was one of those who never left the Prince's side, and as a reward for his loyalty, the Prince gave him the secret recipe for his personal liqueur – all he had of value. It is not known from where the recipe came. It is known, however, that when he was on the run in Scotland, the Prince had a little bottle in his pouch out of which he used to take so many drops every morning and throughout the day, saying that if anything should ail him he hoped he

Prince Charles Edward Stuart.

should cure himself, for he was something of a doctor. It was common in Europe for people to drink elixirs for ailments – usually a strong spirit to which special mixtures of spices and herbs were added to the specific direction of an individual. Despite any clear evidence as to the origins of the liqueur recipe given to MacKinnon by the Prince, it is feasible it was that of his personal elixir.

Although the exact ingredients and quantities that make the Drambuie liqueur of today are a well-guarded secret, there is an idea of what went into its forerunner, as fragments of ancient recipes exist. (There were various recipes with different branches of the MacKinnons.)

The MacKinnons' liqueur remained for personal use until 1871 when John Ross, who owned the inn at Broadford, Skye, persuaded one of the MacKinnons to let him try making it and selling it in the inn. The result was much appreciated by the regulars, two of whom were said to declare it to be *an dram buidheach* – 'the drink that satisfies'.

A kilted Malcolm MacKinnon who commercialised Bonnie Prince Charlie's liqueur recipe.

# Drambuie
## the liqueur you prefer to be offered

*A member of the MacKinnon clan blending rare herbs in the Isle of Skye during the eighteenth century, according to the secret recipe of Drambuie.*

This 1950s' advertisement highlights the origins of Drambuie by portraying a member of the MacKinnon clan blending rare herbs according to the secret recipe in the Isle of Skye during the eighteenth century.

Although in 1893 John Ross's son James registered the trademark 'Drambuie', derived from *an dram buidheach*, there was no commercialisation of the liqueur until 1909. Malcolm MacKinnon, who had left Skye in 1900 to work for the Edinburgh wholesale wine and spirit merchant W. MacBeth and Son, met Eleanor, James Ross's widow, who had moved to Edinburgh after her husband's death. Eleanor had kept the recipe given to her husband by the MacKinnons, and Malcolm thought that the old liqueur might be ideal to revitalise the MacBeth business of which he had become a partner. He therefore reached an

agreement with Mrs Ross to manufacture and sell Drambuie and to have the trademark assigned to MacBeth.

Malcolm was taking a gamble by introducing a new whisky drink when he did. Whisky sales had collapsed when, in his 1909 'People's Budget', Chancellor Lloyd George, a confirmed teetotaller, increased whisky excise duty by a third and taxed distilleries direct for the amount of whisky they produced. So draconian were the increases that one of MacBeth's competitors declared that he might as well close his doors.

While in Drambuie's first year

only 12 cases were sold, demand grew, and from Malcom's initial production of 12 bottles a fortnight, the company progressed to exporting cases to military regiments and expatriate Scots the world over. This was achieved by heavily investing in advertising, which Malcolm had realised was necessary to market a new product. He cleverly focused on the age and the romantic story of the liqueur which he thought would make it distinguished and memorable. Advertisements in trade papers and respected publications such as the *Tatler*, *The Times*, *Punch*, the *Sketch* and the *Bystander* had images of

Bonnie Prince Charlie and Highland scenery accompanied by wording emphasising how Drambuie had been known in the Highlands since 1745 and was only now being offered to a wider public. It was described as 'The Isle of Skye Liqueur'. Malcolm also devised a unique squat bottle intended to make Drambuie stand out among a shelf full of traditional whiskies. (While Malcolm had introduced Drambuie in 1909, the history of the product really began in 1914, when he took over MacBeth's and created the Drambuie Liqueur Company Limited as a separate entity.)

Drambuie was the first liqueur to be accepted in the cellars of the Houses of Parliament as well as into those of the royal household at Buckingham Palace. By the end of the First World War every British officers' mess and naval wardroom had its stock of Drambuie, and in the United States sales soared when the era of Prohibition ended. (The war actually helped sales of Drambuie as it was the only liqueur available in Britain, trade routes from the continent having been closed.)

In 1937, the Drambuie Liqueur Company Limited took over the old-established whisky blender Innes and Grieve whose premises were at 12 York Place, Edinburgh. Drambuie's production was moved into these premises, but that was all that changed. The quality of the product remained true to the original recipe, which is kept in a safe-deposit box in an Edinburgh bank. The recipe for the essence is still a closely guarded secret, and today a female member of the Mackinnon family blends the ingredients in a private laboratory. When ready, the essence is transferred into custom-built

containers that are double padlocked. Only one employee is entrusted with a key, and that person is responsible for the blending of the essence with the whisky base. Drambuie is the only traditional liqueur to use a base of 100 per cent aged Scotch whiskies.

Drambuie again had a monopoly in the liqueur market in Britain during the Second World War, as continental brands were unavailable, as they had been in the previous war. Supplies were available in pubs and hotels as well as in regimental messes, and as the Allied forces gathered in the south of England in 1944, there was sufficient for the troops. By this time, Malcolm MacKinnon was seriously ill, and in May 1945, at the age of sixty-two, he died.

After the war there was an increased worldwide demand for Drambuie, and in 1959 a new production facility was opened at Easter Road, Edinburgh, and although the plant was technologically advanced the herbs and spices were still collected and mixed by one person, Gina MacKinnon, Malcolm's widow and the chairman of the company. (Gina said that the reason she was the guardian of the recipe and not her son was simple – women are better at keeping secrets than men.)

Growth continued, and in 1969 work began on another new plant at Kirkliston, eight miles west of Edinburgh. While it was the most

advanced and sophisticated liqueur-processing plant in the world, the production process was a careful balance between technology and traditional values, including the time-honoured practice of rinsing out bottles with a jet of pure whisky before use.

By the 1970s, however, the whisky industry was in turmoil, with even a successful brand like Drambuie fighting to maintain sales. As Malcolm MacKinnon had done years before, heavily investing in marketing and promotion was the solution, and advertisements geared to an international customer base, such as the luxurious art-deco-style series with the slogan 'It Travels Well', appeared in magazines and Sunday newspaper supplements. These successful advertisements, along with

The brilliant Nectar advertisement showing a hummingbird hovering to capture the elusive drop of Drambuie.

classic and contemporary cocktails, like the 'Rusty Nail' – a combination of quality Scotch and Drambuie. Its sophisticated strength and subtlety is superb over cubed or crushed ice, a combination promoted in a sequel to the hapless butler television advertisement, this time featuring actor Robert Powell at his Venetian dinner party requesting ice from the Alps to add to the Drambuie. Speed skiers and powerboats whizz it to the butler, who, with a great flourish, puts it into a glass ice bucket that is promptly shattered by the cold.

Most of the Drambuie Liqueur Company's sales are to the export market. The product is truly international and can be found in over 200 countries, in duty-free outlets, planes, boats and trains. If you travel abroad, therefore, you can enjoy Drambuie before departure, in transit and at your journey's end. Further, if you happen to be invited to the Vatican it has been available there since 1992.

As by the twenty-first century the Kirkliston plant was in need of updating, Drambuie formed a supply chain partnership with Glenmorangie, a distiller of premium malt whiskies. A new company, Glenaird Ltd, was formed to handle Glenmorangie's and Drambuie's supply chains, and in the summer of 2001 Drambuie's bottling operations were transferred to Glenmorangie's plant at Broxburn. Throughout the process, both companies emphasised that they intend to retain their independence.

Drambuie's head office, Hillwood House, had been Malcom MacKinnon's old home, which was sold to meet death duties. His

A 2002 advertisement for Drambuie on ice.

the brilliant 'Nectar' one, showing a hummingbird hovering to capture the elusive drop of Drambuie, gave the liqueur a sophisticated rather than a homespun image.

Television advertising did not begin until 1990, humour being the approach adopted. In the first advertisement, the clumsy butler who drops the Drambuie sets in motion an intercontinental journey for a replacement, which he promptly drops again to the exasperation of actor Robert Hardy.

Drambuie breaks all language barriers and is the quintessential Scottish liqueur, epitomising quality, refinement and taste. It mixes well, making it the perfect partner in

grandsons bought it in 1998, and the Drambuie coat of arms and the Scottish saltire fly from its tower. It is in Hillwood, in a small locked private laboratory, that the ancient recipe is mixed to the exacting standards implemented by Malcolm MacKinnon in 1909 in his gloomy cellar in Union Street.

The extraordinary Drambuie story will be kept alive as the recipe is handed down to future generations of the family, and as the Gaelic motto on every bottle of Drambuie says: *Cuimhnich An Tabhartas Prionnsa* – 'Remember the Gift of the Prince'.

*Information and illustrations courtesy of Drambuie.*

The name of Kirkcaldy has become synonymous with the production of linoleum, and at the forefront of the industry that brought prosperity to the Lang Toun is the floor-covering giant Forbo-Nairn Limited, or Nairn's as it has been to Kirkcaldy folk since 1847 when Michael Nairn started building the 'Scottish Floor Cloth Manufactory'.

In 1828, at the age of twenty-eight, Michael Nairn, from a long-established Fife family, started up a canvas-weaving business in Coal Wynd, Kirkcaldy. His wares were mainly used for sailcloth and as well as selling them in Britain he exported to the corners of the world. Bleached canvas went to India, Canada, America, Jamaica, Australia, Mauritius and even Greenland. Also to America went oilcloth – canvas that has been waterproofed.

Times were changing, however, and, with the arrival of steam power, so was the shipping industry. The days of sail were numbered, and sales to floorcloth manufacturers gradually played a larger role in Michael Nairn's operations until, by 1844, he was supplying canvas to two dozen floorcloth firms, two-thirds of the total number in existence. The canvas was used as backing for the floorcloth.

Although developed in the seventeenth century, floorcloth was made mainly in London, with no factories outside England. Michael Nairn decided to change that. After visiting one of his customers, John Hare of Bristol, he returned to Kirkcaldy in a thoughtful mood. As he was already equipped to make floorcloth canvas, why should he not produce floorcloth? As the manufacturing process took as long as ten months from start to finish, however, it would be a tremendous gamble as he would have to start from scratch by building a factory, buying materials, paying workers and keeping everything going with no money coming in for two years.

When Michael began to look for partners among his friends so that he could set up his floorcloth factory, they all thought he was mad and declined to be involved. Nevertheless, in 1847, he started work on a new factory on a site at the top of a cliff at Pathhead near Ravenscraig Castle. (The site, in fact, had been carefully chosen as it was five minutes' walk from the new station at Sinclairtown on the Edinburgh, Perth and Dundee railway.) When completed, sceptical locals dubbed the factory 'Nairn's Folly'. Little did they know, however, that a completely new manufacturing era had arrived. Even Michael, ambitious though he was, could hardly have had an inkling that he was laying the foundations of a business that would reach out across the world and would still be thriving in the twenty-first century.

In 1849 the first floorcloth was ready for sale. Making it was an involved process. Two men wove a

Michael Nairn.

Hand-printing loft for floorcloth. This illustration gives an indication of what a hand-printing department was like in the nineteenth century. The boys shown were known as 'tear boys'. This name, variously spelt, was taken from the old word 'teer', which meant to spread, to plaster, to daub. This exactly described the work of the boys, who spread paint over a large pad composed of three-ply plaiding covered by a piece of canvas. (Michael Nairn had been supplying these pads to English floorcloth factories for years.) The name 'tear boy' was not confined to floorcloth making. It was current in other industries where a similar block-printing process was used.

canvas web 150 yards long by 8 yards wide in a fortnight. The web was then cut into 25-yard lengths that were nailed taut on to vertical frames to stretch before sizing and painting. (The frame supports were made from whole pine trees, normally used for making ships' masts.) There was no question of buying in paint – the workers made their own. Combinations of ochres and leads were ground to a powder and mixed with linseed oil and various other ingredients and then ground again between a pair of millstones. Several coats of the thick paint were daubed on to the canvas with brushes and spread with trowels into a thin film. Once each

coat of paint was dry, it was rubbed smooth with pumice stone. The processes took months to complete as the only way of drying the paint was by ventilation through the factory's huge 41-foot-high windows. The first floor was 47 feet high, so 90-foot lengths of linoleum could be suspended in giant U shapes to dry.

Then came the printing. Designs in 18-inch square blocks were printed repeatedly, with additional colours or elaborate patterns being overprinted with different blocks. For more elaborate patterns between two and three thousand single applications of printing blocks were required. The setting of the block in its exact place

needed great care for it was often impossible to undo an error after the impression had been made, which is why Michael Nairn employed only men of 'sober and steady habits'.

Michael Nairn received a severe blow when he took part in the Great Industrial Exhibition of 1851 in the Crystal Palace, Hyde Park, London. All the floorcloth manufacturers were derided for producing monotonous and unoriginal designs. Taking the criticism to heart – and to be fair some manufacturers had been churning out the same designs for half a century or so – Michael devoted much effort to remedying the situation, which paid off (although he did not see it as he died in 1858) for the company's wares received acclaim at the 1862 World's Fair. More acclaim came at the 1867 Paris Exhibition when a Nairn design was described as 'the most magnificent work of the kind ever produced'. By then Michael Nairn's son, Michael Barker Nairn, was running the company.

For some time floorcloth had been criticised for being too cold underfoot, and in 1863, Yorkshireman Frederick Walton registered a patent for linoleum, a warmer and more resilient alternative. As the main constituent was the oil of flax or linseed oil, it was named linoleum from the Latin *linum* (flax) and *oleum* (oil).

Although linoleum was initially made in one-yard widths, making it in many respects inferior to the much wider floorcloth, Michael

A colourful and intricate hand-printed floorcloth design from 1880.

'On the floor of this drawing-room is Nairn Super Parquet Inlaid Linoleum. It is not only artistic, hardwearing and resilient, but, when polished, makes an admirable dancing floor.' This captioned one of the many pictures used to illustrate a booklet from The House of Nairn, produced to mark the company's participation in the 1924 British Empire Exhibition. The parquet design flooring was very expensive at 10/6d. per square yard. The booklet also contains a number of photographs showing what was then some of the most modern flooring production machinery in the world.

Barker Nairn believed it had a future. He bided his time until Walton's patent ran out, and in 1877, having constructed a purpose-built factory, started producing linoleum, which is when Kirkcaldy got the first whiff of its famous 'queer-like' smell, so notorious that it was immortalised in a poem including the lines:

I'll sune be ringin' ma Grandma's
    bell,
She'll cry 'Come in, my laddie!'
For I ken masel' by the queeer-like
    smell,
That the next stop's Kirkcaldy.

The poem, 'The Boy In The Train', written by Mary Campbell Smith in 1913 for the Merchiston School Magazine, tells of the train journey of a schoolboy who is travelling to visit his grandmother. The waiting area in Kirkcaldy Station has the rhyme cut into lino by Forbo-Nairn.

The cause of the 'queer-like' smell was the oxidisation of linseed, the raw material for linoleum. Scrim cloth was hung in sheds and boiled linseed oil was flooded over the scrim and left to oxidise. This process was repeated until the sheets of solidified oil had reached a thickness of one inch or more, by

which time they were ready to be ground up and mixed with powdered cork and pigments. The granulated mixture was then compressed between huge rollers, called calendars, to produce a seamless sheet of single colour linoleum.

At first the linoleum was made in two-yard widths and had to be hand-printed, then in 1881 Nairn was the first to produce it in four-yard widths. The printed designs were still a drawback, but in 1895 a major development came with the introduction of inlaid designs, which meant the pattern went right

This image of 1968 is the front page of the first Cushionflor brochure.

through the linoleum.

When Michael Barker Nairn – by then Sir Michael – died in 1915, the company was an international concern with factories in France, Germany anc America, and with orders from as far away as Siberia.

The 1920s saw an important development – the manufacture of Congoleum, the main difference between it and linoleum being that, while the latter had a hessian canvas backing, Congoleum had a cheaper tough bituminised felt base, making it affordable to those for whom linoleum was too expensive. Prices then ranged from 3/2d. per square yard for an average quality floorcloth to 10/6d. per square yard for parquet flooring.

As during the Second World War, only a small quantity of linoleum was made under government contracts, Nairn's workers began turning out tarpaulins and bituminised felt for covering windows and doorways blown out by bombing raids. They also made fuel tanks for Halifax bombers and torpedoes and bombs, such as the 10-ton Grand Slams that were used for smashing submarine pens and penetrating the armoured decks of battleships.

Although in the 1950s Nairn successfully introduced Lino Tiles, by the following decade linoleum was out of favour. PVC and vinyl floor coverings had come on to the market, as had cheap tufted carpets manufactured by companies such as Cyril Lord whose adverts told everyone that 'this was the luxury you could afford'. Everyone wanted wall-to-wall carpeting, and Britain became the most carpeted country in the world per capita.

Sales of printed vinyl kept Nairn going, but it was an invention by American subsidiary Congoleum-Nairn – Cushionflor – a cushioned vinyl, which, when launched in 1967, proved to be the company's salvation as by 1972 it was Britain's most popular resilient floor-covering.

Cushionflor did not mean the end for linoleum – Nairn continued to manufacture it despite annual sales having fallen from 21 million square metres in 1965 to 1.78 million by 1981. Help, however, was around the corner in the form of Swiss based Forbo SA, which had faith in linoleum and produced it in Holland. Forbo wanted a UK base and when Unilever, which owned Nairn, decided to sell up in 1985, Forbo-Nairn was born, giving Kirkcaldy's linoleum industry a new lease of life. Because linoleum is a generic term, not a brand name, Forbo-Nairn's product is known as Marmoleum.

Environmentally friendly

Aquajet floor in the Banking Hall of The Royal Bank of Scotland, Dundas House, St Andrews Square, Edinburgh. Note that the design echoes that of the elaborate ceiling. The Marmoleum was printed before the floor was installed.

Marmoleum is the latest in designer flooring. Using aquajet cutters, floor design is limited only by the customer's imagination. Any image can be created, like Sonic the Hedgehog for Sega World in London. Other commercial customers go for more discreet company logos. Children's hospitals have teddies and cartoons, and Forbo-Nairn's own offices are an eye-catching advertisement for the company. Imagination, flair and humour all come into play with Marmoleum floors, indicating office designations and demarcations.

With two such quality products as Cushionflor and Marmoleum, Forbo-Nairn, the oldest manufac-turer of resilient floor-coverings in the world, should go from strength to strength. Michael Nairn's gamble certainly paid off.

*Information and illustrations courtesy of Forbo-Nairn Archive.*

# GLENFIDDICH

The story of Glenfiddich, the world's best-selling malt whisky and the world's first single malt whisky, is fascinating. The distillery, which has been continuously owned and managed by the Grant family for five generations, began with William Grant, born in 1839, the son of a Dufftown tailor who had served with Wellington in the Penninsular Wars.

The young William Grant was first a cattle-herder, then an apprentice cobbler and finally a clerk at the local lime works before joining the nearby Mortlach distillery in 1866 as book-keeper and later manager. During his twenty years at Mortlach, William learned all he could about distilling as he had decided that his future lay in establishing his own distillery. To this end, the family saved every penny it could – William from his £200 a year salary, his wife from frugal housekeeping, his children from university prizes and, in the case of his eldest son, John, from his teacher's salary. William had nine children – two daughters and seven sons – all of whom were allowed to study, unusual for the times. Among the family were a teacher, a lawyer and two doctors.

After years of saving, William had a lucky break in 1886. When the Cardhu Distillery at Knockando decided to install new plant, he acquired the old plant for the bargain price of £119 19s. 0d. He

Glenfiddich Distillery.

Founder of Glenfiddich,
William Grant with Glenfiddich Distillery
in the background.

knew that, although the stills and condensers were second-hand, they were still capable of producing an excellent dram. William then chose a site close to Dufftown in the field of Glenfiddich ('the valley of the deer') for his distillery. Water was to be drawn from the Robbie Dhu Springs in the Conval Hills, a secret location that legend says was shown to William by a priest.

Working seven days a week, with just the help of a mason, a carpenter and the advice of an architect, William and his family built their distillery for little more than £700. Named Glenfiddich, the first whisky ran from its stills on Christmas Day 1887. As well as helping to finance the distillery, William's children helped run it, even his three youngest sons who were still at school preparing for entrance to Aberdeen University.

The bulk of Glenfiddich's whisky was sold for blending. It was also sold as being suitable for medicinal purposes, the justification being, according to the company, that every stage of it was supervised by a qualified doctor – William's fourth son, Alex, who was the head stillman. His younger brother George was maltman and Charles was the brewer.

A big breakthrough came when Smith's Glenlivet Distillery caught fire and Glenfiddich was able to step in and meet an order that Glenlivet could not fulfil. After that the company prospered, and by 1892 it was building a second distillery at nearby Balvenie.

By diversifying into blending and dealing directly with retailers, the Grant family survived the collapse in 1889 of its main customer, Pattison of Leith, one of the largest blenders

and wholesalers in the country and whose bankruptcy led to a great crisis in the industry. Among the blends introduced, the most successful was Standfast which became so popular that an export market was developed. Standfast (now Family Reserve) was named after the Clan Grant battle cry of 'Stand fast, Craigellachie'.

When William Grant sent both his son Charles and son-in-law Charles Gordon to Glasgow to establish a base from which to wholesale and export the William Grant blended whisky brand, it took Charles Gordon 181 calls to make his first sale. Later he travelled to the Far East, Australia and New Zealand while John Grant travelled to Canada and the United States. Their efforts were rewarded, and by the beginning of the First World War William Grant was selling its blends worldwide through sixty agencies in thirty countries.

Despite going blind, William Grant carried on the business he and his family had worked so hard to build up, and he was eighty-three when he died in 1923.

With whisky in plentiful supply

after the Second World War, the company needed to give the William Grant brand a distinctive characteristic that would make it stand out on the shelf, so in 1957 it pioneered the now familiar Glenfiddich triangular bottle.

Most Glenfiddich whisky was sold for blending, that is until 1963 when a courageous decision was made to market Glenfiddich as a single malt whisky. It was a gamble, as single malt whisky had never been generally promoted as it was considered too strong in flavour and body. Glenfiddich, however, was a delicately flavoured light-bodied whisky and, packaged in its triangular green bottle with a large label showing a stag, 'The Monarch of the Glen', the heraldic animal of the Grants, it was a success, and by 1974 almost 120,000 cases were being exported. Glenfiddich created the malt whisky market.

Unlike any other producer, all the water used at Glenfiddich is from a single source – the Robbie Dhu Springs – hence the marketing slogan 'a single source of inspiration'. (The company owns the whole hillside in order to protect the

Glenfiddich stills, which have not changed in shape or size from the originals. Even the original dents incurred on the journey from Cardhu to Glenfiddich were carefully replicated in case the spirit would be affected.

precious water supply which is soft and slightly peaty.) Split between two still houses, the 28 pot spirit stills are unusually small, being replicas of those William Grant bought second-hand from Cardhu in 1886. In fact, William Grant would find little changed at Glenfiddich since his time. The same raw materials are still used in the making of the whisky because to alter a single detail might affect the taste and quality of Glenfiddich, something the company is not prepared to risk.

Glenfiddich Special Reserve, the world's most famous single malt whisky, is matured for a minimum of twelve years in oak casks. It is the only malt in the Highlands to be distilled, matured and bottled at its own distillery.

Glenfiddich also produces Solera Reserve 15 Year Old, the first malt whisky in the world to be made using a Solera system, traditionally associated with sherry production, which enables malt whisky matured in different types of casks to be married together. The character of Glenfiddich Ancient Reserve 18 Year Old comes from long years of maturation in Oloroso sherry casks and traditional bourbon casks. Gran Reserva 21 Year Old resurrects a lost nineteenth-century tradition of maturing Scotch whisky in rum casks. Caoran Reserve 21 Year Old (named from the Gaelic for peat ember) was developed to re-create the flavour of Glenfiddich whisky distilled during the 1930s and 40s, when, because of war-induced coal shortages, more peat than usual was used on the fires to dry the barley, resulting in a delicious smoky-flavoured malt.

In March 2003 an independent panel of 75 whisky experts across three continents awarded Glenfiddich Rare Collection 40 Year Old a gold medal and the accolade of being the best single malt in the world. Glenfiddich 1937 is the oldest single malt Scotch in the world and sells at £10,000 per bottle. Only 61 bottles were produced. Glenfiddich 50 Year Old is available at £5,000 per bottle.

William Grant & Sons has

Advertisement from The Glenfiddich Guide to the Seven Deadly Sins series – 4 'Lust'.

always been innovative and skilful in packaging its products, starting with the introduction of the now familiar triangular bottle which was unconventional at the time. It was also the first to put its products in tubes and gift tins, with its Glenfiddich Clan tin series being the best-selling form of gift presentation in the world.

Historically, Glenfiddich advertisements are different from other whisky campaigns – for example, the 'Recto-Verso' campaign mounted in France in 1989 and the surreal 'Time' series for the UK and Europe introduced in the first half of the 1990s. There was controversy at the end of 2002, however, when television advertisements that changed the pronunciation of Glenfiddich to please English consumers were introduced. Instead of the final syllable having the proper Scottish soft 'ich' sound it was given a hard 'ick' sound – Glenfiddick. After complaints, the company reverted to the softer pronunciation for the English and Scottish advertisements, which show a stag roaming city streets, but those to be shown in the United States kept the hard 'ick' sound as it was felt it was more global and generic.

Glenfiddich was the first distillery in Scotland to open a visitor centre. Apart from guided tours and whisky tastings, the centre, opened in 1969, offers audiovisual presentations and multilingual commentaries to cater for the large number of overseas visitors, at least a thousand of them Japanese. Open all year round, the centre, which has a shop, has around 80,000 visitors a year, and on 4 August 1987 it welcomed its one-millionth visitor – Ronald Peterson from Albany in New York State.

Since 1886 the single-minded dedication of William Grant & Sons Ltd, one of Scotland's few independently owned and family-run distillers, has resulted in it producing the finest single malt Scotch whisky in the world. 'Made without Compromise' appears on the label of Special Reserve, the world's best-selling single malt whisky available in about 200 countries. These words sum up the philosophy of the company.

Information and illustrations courtesy of William Grant & Sons.

In the UK, the bottled water market is worth £1.7 billion, with 2.19 billion litres consumed in 2007. More than half of the adult population drinks bottled water, a very different story from when mineral waters were considered medicines, which they were until 1833, when they were exempted from levies and could be drunk for refreshment as well as for medicinal purposes.

Formed in 1979, Highland Spring is the leading UK-produced brand of bottled water and the number one spring water. Its home is the village of Blackford in Perthshire, renowned for its water for centuries. King James IV stopped there in 1488 and paid the, then, vast sum of 12 shillings (60p) for ale made from local water.

Above. Highland Spring Sparkling Water.

Below. The Ochil Hills in summer.

Highland Spring's water, which is low in minerals, salts and nitrates, comes from a natural underground source under the Ochil Hills, where no farming, agricultural spraying, building or habitation are permitted within the 2000-acre catchment area. The land has been kept free from pesticides and pollution for over twenty years.

The weather on the Ochil Hills is harsh. Even on a mild autumn day, the temperature at the top of the Hills can drop to minus zero, and when it rains, it rains sideways. Although every drop helps to replenish the reservoirs deep underground, there is no problem with supply as Highland Spring only uses a fraction of the water in the hillside. The water, regarded by

Children enjoying a drink of Highland Spring water after an energetic game of tennis.

Highland Spring at the gym.

experts as among the finest mineral waters in the world, takes about fifteen years to filter through the basalt and sandstone strata to boreholes lined with stainless steel, which allow the water to be gently pumped to the surface and then down to the bottling plant. Mineral water must be bottled at source, and at Highland Spring it is bottled within hours of leaving the ground. It is untouched by human hand and is delivered to consumers exactly as nature intended, with nothing added or taken away, apart from the addition of $CO_2$ for its sparkling range.

Research shows that British consumers view Scotland as having the purest water in the UK, and Highland Spring's stylised tartan packaging highlights the product's Scottish provenance.

In April 2001, Highland Spring acquired its Blackford neighbour, Gleneagles Spring Water Company, an upmarket brand of natural mineral water with an award-winning stylish glass bottle. The water is bottled at source from the Gleneagles valley in the Ochil Hills. Popular in exclusive hotels and restaurants at home and abroad, it is the only natural mineral water brand stocked by the Scotch Whisky Heritage Centre. The company also owns Watermedia, the UK market leader in the niche private sector label.

Despite a growth in the popularity of bottled water amongst youngsters, carbonated drinks remain their most popular choice, and in 2007 the company launched the first sparkling kids' water, Highland Spring for Kids, now the leading brand of children's bottled water.

Still water accounts for around 72 percent of bottled water sales, and Highland Spring out-performed the bottled water market in 2007. It consolidated its number two position by extending its lead over the third largest brand Volvic, while edging closer to Evian. In the sparkling market, Highland Spring is the market leader, and it sells five times more than its nearest competitor, Perrier.

Highland Spring is a major supporter of UK sport and a long-term sponsor of many national and international events, such as the Johnnie Walker Golf Championship and the Paralympic World Cup. It is the exclusive beverage sponsor of Andy Murray, Britain's number one

Colourful advertisement from 2005 showing a bottle of Highland Spring water depicted as a stylised thistle.

tennis player, who displays the brand logo on his shirt sleeve and who drinks Highland Spring as part of his dietary regime. It is also the official bottled water supplier to the World Snooker Association and sponsor of team Highland Spring, that consists of 14 snooker players, including Stephen Hendry, Ronnie O'Sullivan and Ken Doherty. The Highland Spring logo and tartan appears on the players' waistcoats.

As people are becoming more aware of the health benefits of a high water intake, the sharp rise in global demand for bottled water looks set to continue. To facilitate increased demand, Highland Spring was reclassified as a 'spring water' in 2007 to enable it to manage its water resources more efficiently and to give access to at least another 100 million litres of water a year, without putting stress on the catchment area or local environment.

**SOME FACTS ABOUT WATER**
- Water makes up about 75% of the human body and our brain tissue consists of up to 85% water.
- We can live for weeks without food but only a few days without water.
- Dehydration is a common cause of minor health problems – lethargy, headaches, constipation.

*Information and illustrations courtesy of Highland Spring*

Irn-Bru is the leading brand of soft drink manufacturer A. G. Barr plc. Known as 'Scotland's other national drink' and a favourite hangover cure for Glaswegians, the recipe is a secret known to only two board members and is kept in a bank vault for safety. What makes the recipe unique is that while other carbonated fruit drinks typically have at most two or three flavouring ingredients, Irn-Bru has thirty-two, which is why it has proved impossible to copy.

The Barr story began in 1875 when Robert Barr added a soft drinks business to the cork-cutting operations established by his father in Falkirk in 1830. In 1887 Robert's son, also Robert, started his own soft drinks business in Great Eastern Road, Glasgow, later renamed Gallowgate. Five years after getting his business up and running, however, Robert moved to Ireland, leaving his brother Andrew as sole proprietor, at which time the company became A. G. Barr & Co.

In 1901 Robert Barr, Falkirk, and A. G. Barr & Co., Glasgow, jointly launched Iron Brew, just one of many such named products – a refreshing mixed-flavour drink for which all the manufacturers had their own recipes. Other soft drinks manufactured by Barr included 'Old Scotch' ginger beer, orangeade, lemonade, soda water and raspberry cider. All drinks were packaged in returnable glass bottles.

When Iron Brew was introduced, A. G. Barr employed around 200 people in Glasgow and 150 horses were required to cope with deliveries. As it is today, advertising was important, and Andrew Barr gave his lorries an eye-catching white and gold livery carrying the company name in large clear letters.

Iron Brew's first label depicted

Above. Early Iron Brew label featuring Highland athlete Adam Brown.

Left. Andrew Greig Barr, from whom the company took its name. He died suddenly after contracting the glanders virus. He was only thirty-one years of age. He saw the launch of Iron Brew and instigated the formation of the limited company A. G. Barr & Co. Ltd, which took place in 1904. Sadly, he did not live long enough to see his plans for the business come to fruition.

A late 1930s' example of point-of-sale material used for 'Iron Brew'.

The Cambridge rower label that in 1922 replaced the Highland athlete.

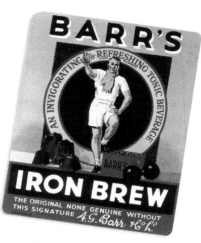

Adam Brown, a famous Highland athlete from Shotts, holding aloft a glass of Barr's Iron Brew. As William Barr, chairman 1909–1931, was a devotee of strong man George Sandow's body-building techniques, Barr's marketing focused on associating sporting and athletic prowess with its products. In 1904 Donald Dinnie, all-round Champion Athlete of the World, endorsed the product by stating 'I can recommend Iron Brew to all who wish to aspire to athletic fame.' Willie Lyon of Celtic said the product was 'The best restorative for any athlete', and in 1938, Scotland's greatest boxer, Benny Lynch, was paid £3 for his testimonial, which repeated that of Donald Dinnie. The Highland athlete on the label was replaced by a Cambridge rower in 1922.

At the start of the Second World War Iron Brew remained on sale, but in 1942, because of a shortage of raw materials like sugar and paper, the government restricted the industry to a number of manufacturers. Each one authorised to continue was given a number. Barr's was 'No. 6'. However, the companies were allowed to manufacture only standard drinks,

and as Iron Brew was not
recognised as one of these,
production of that flavour ceased.
Barr was allocated a ration of sugar
and given six recipes which, to make
the sugar go further, specified half
sugar and half saccharin as the
sweetening content. The company
advertised the loss of Iron Brew
during the war as 'One of the
hardships of the war effort'! Because
of paper shortages, Barr's own labels
were downsized in 1947 when all
manufacturers were again permitted
to sell their own brands.

When, after the war, it was
proposed to introduce new food-
labelling regulations that stipulated
that brand names should be literally
true, there was concern that the
name Iron Brew would no longer be
permitted. Just as Ginger Ale was
not ale and American Cream Soda
was neither made in America nor
contained cream, Iron Brew was not
brewed, although it did contain
0.125 mg of iron per fluid ounce.
Chairman Robert Barr's brilliant idea
to get round this legislation was to
use a phonetic version of the
generic name and in 1946 'Irn-Bru'
was registered as the trade name
for the company's No. 1 brand. As it
happened, the new labelling
regulations did not come into effect
until 1964 when they were
moderated by a 'grandfather rule'
that meant a company could
continue to use a name that was
not literally true if it had been in use
for thirty years. By then, however,
everyone was used to Irn-Bru and
there was no point in changing back
to Iron Brew.

'Ba-Bru' says —

# BARR'S IRON BREW

*"all enjoy this Big favourite"*

3D

The Barr story is not one of spectacular growth but of steady expansion, careful acquisition and persistent specialisation. In 1954, the company set out to 'conquer' England by acquiring John Hollows, a small company based in Bradford, and an advertising campaign to introduce Irn-Bru to the north of England was launched. In 1959, one single family business was finally created when A. G. Barr & Co. Ltd took over the original Robert Barr business in Falkirk.

Barr's products were sold in Edinburgh for the first time in only 1963. When Robert Barr had set up his soft drinks business in Falkirk in 1875, Mr Dunbar of the Dunbar soft drinks company in Edinburgh helped him to do so, leading to a gentleman's agreement that neither company would sell their products in each other's territory. This agreement, which lasted for over eighty-five years, ended only when Dunbar bought a soft drinks business in Kirkcaldy where Barr was already established.

In 1965 A. G. Barr & Co. Ltd was floated on the Stock Exchange, with 500,000 ordinary shares being offered for sale at 9s. 3d. Applications for over two million shares were received. After the flotation, the company expanded its business south with the acquisition of soft drink companies in Sunderland and Atherton near Manchester. Special Irn-Bru labels were produced for the English market. Profits were boosted in 1970 when Barr introduced the first ring-pull can ends in the UK. Later the company was the first major soft drinks manufacturer in the UK to adopt stay-on tabs on cans.

Barr's breakthrough nationally came in 1972 when it acquired Tizer Ltd, the proprietors of the famous household brand Tizer – The Appetizer. Expansion continued in the 1980s with the purchase of Globe Soft Drinks of Edinburgh and Mandora St. Clements with factories in Mansfield and Evesham. Irn-Bru arrived in Russia in 1998 as a result of a franchise arrangement with a bottler in Moscow, and it is also available in other parts of the world, e.g. Malta, Spain, Canada, Australia and Cyprus.

Innovative, witty and vigorous advertising has always played a large part in Irn-Bru's success, and while early advertising focused on associating sporting and athletic prowess with the company's products, the 1930s saw the introduction of the company's well-loved campaign that introduced generations of Scots to Barr's Iron Brew. It was the 'Adventures of Ba-Bru and Sandy', two boys, one a turbaned Indian, one a tam-o-shantered, kilted Scot, forever on the hunt for Barr's Iron Brew. ('Ba-Bru' was inspired by the character Sabu in Rudyard Kipling's book *Sabu the Elephant Boy*.) The Adventures of Ba-Bru and Sandy appeared weekly in newspapers and became the longest-running commercial advertising cartoon in history, lasting until the early 1970s.

Although Iron Brew vanished from the shelves during the Second World War, to keep its memory alive the company continued to run the Ba-Bru and Sandy cartoons. In 1947, the cartoons carried the phonetic version of 'Irn-Bru' for the first time. In the 1950s England was introduced to Ba-Bru and Sandy, and a new neon sign of Ba-Bru was sited on top of Central Station in Glasgow (since removed). The first Barr TV advertisement (1964) was based on a Ba-Bru and Sandy cartoon. Unfortunately, no copy of the advert exists in the company's archives.

The well-loved Ba-Bru and Sandy gave way to a more sophisticated style of advertising in the mid-1970s – the highly successful poster and TV campaign that coined the famous catchphrases 'Your other national drink' and 'Made in Scotland from girders'. Boys with ginger hair were used while the metal girders symbolised the iron. Characters symbolising strength, such as 'Popeye', were also used. Although these campaigns ended in the 1990s, people still remember the famous phrases. Barr's sugar tankers, painted to look like giant Irn-Bru cans, bore the slogan 'Don't drink more than eighty gallons a day or you'll rust.'

Not all the company's adverts were received so well, however. 1995 saw the introduction of an award-winning poster campaign that caused amusement and controversy. Captions were suggestive, and one advert showing a cow dreaming of being a burger was named the most offensive of 1998. The poster attracted almost 600 complaints.

In 2000, the humorous poster format was translated to TV. Each advert featured an amusing tale of people's desire for Irn-Bru. (The same format as Ba-Bru and Sandy, who were always searching for 'Iron Brew' as it was then.) However, the most unforgettable TV advert has to be the one transmitted in 2001

showing a little old lady in her motorised invalid scooter, a balaclava pulled over her face, charging her way into a supermarket. Deliberately, she crashes through a stack of Irn-Bru much of which ends up in her scooter basket. She then hurtles out of the store door, her scooter skidding on two wheels. A classic advertisement, but one that was criticised by some disabled groups as being 'in bad taste.' A close second was the 'Grandad' advert in which granddad and his grandson are sitting together, grandson drinking from a can of Irn-Bru. Grandad asks for a sip and grandson hands the can over. Grandad whips out his false teeth and takes an enormous slurp from the can. He then hands it back to his

grandson who, in disgust, indicates that grandad should keep it. Grandad puts his teeth in, genteelly sips from the can and then laughs. His ploy worked. He got to finish the can.

Irn-Bru is as Scottish as tartan and shortbread and is among the most popular Scottish products craved by ex-pats the world over. It was 100 years old in 2001 and is the No. 1 grocery brand in Scotland. From being just one of hundreds of soft drinks businesses in Scotland in 1875, A. G. Barr is the UK's No. 1 independent soft drinks business with nearly 1,000 employees working from 16 sites.

*Information and illustrations courtesy of A. G. Barr p.l.c.*

An advertisement from the mid-1970s featuring 'Popeye' consuming a can of Irn-Bru to give him strength instead of his customary spinach.

An amusing, but suggestive, poster from 2001.

# JOHNNIE WALKER WHISKY

In 1820 John Walker, son of an Ayrshire farmer, opened a small grocery, wine and spirit shop in Kilmarnock. He became a blending pioneer and was soon selling his own stocks of whisky all over the surrounding area. From the beginning, John's blend had a high reputation that spread throughout Scotland and eventually into England. His son Alexander joined him in 1856 and moved the company in the direction of wholesale rather than retail trade. John Walker died in 1857.

While the blend 'Johnnie Walker's Old Highland Whisky' was begun in the 1850s, the label was not copyrighted until 1867. Old Highland, which became known as 'Walker's Kilmarnock Whisky', was a long way in character and taste from modern Scotch, but it was in its day a most successful product – extremely rich and peaty with a very strong taste. The secret blend recipe still exists.

Go-ahead Alexander reached overseas markets by entrusting his whisky to the captains of ships sailing out of Glasgow who sold it on commission at the best price they could get. He also took advantage of Kilmarnock's reputation as a carpet and textile centre to introduce the visiting English buyers to the delights of his whisky. Having done that, he made sure they could get their supplies at home by opening a London office in 1880.

Silhouette of John Walker, who founded the business that went on to produce the world's best-selling Scotch whisky, Johnnie Walker Red Label.

When Alexander Walker died in 1889, Johnnie Walker & Sons Limited was one of the most important whisky firms in the world. After Alexander's death, his three sons, George, John and Alexander, took over. In 1890, when John Walker sailed for Australia where he opened the company's first overseas subsidiary, local man James Stevenson joined the firm and went on to play an outstanding part in its growth and expansion.

As demand for whisky was soaring worldwide, to increase production and to maintain the quality of its product the firm needed its own distillery. In 1893, therefore, it acquired the once illegal distillery of Cardhu in Speyside, so highly rated by the Walker brothers' father that he used its malt whisky as the base around which he developed his Old Highland blend. At the same time, a new director was acquired, John Cumming, son of Elizabeth Cumming who sold Cardhu to the Walkers. The purchase guaranteed the firm the supply of the finest Highland whiskies that it needed for its blends, a fact it emphasised: 'The purchase of the distillery will give us a thorough command of our manufacture from the very start and give us absolute certainty about the quality of the principal components of our blend.'

In the early 1900s, the firm decided to replace its two principal blends, Johnnie Walker Very Special Old Highland Whisky and Johnnie Walker Extra Special Old Highland Whisky, with new ones that would build on the traditional taste and quality but have fresh dimensions of complexity and subtlety. To this end, Alexander Walker, who was a master blender, and two blending experts set to work and produced the famous Johnnie Walker Red Label and Johnnie Walker Black Label whiskies. It is interesting to note that Johnnie Walker whiskies taste exactly the same today as they did when created. Buy a bottle of Red Label or Black Label and you will experience the flavour that so excited Alexander Walker and his co-blenders when it was first sampled. Why change a winning formula?

In the case of Red Label, all the ingredient whiskies were older than the three years that was legally necessary for a whisky to be described as Scotch. With Black Label, Alexander turned to older stocks of whisky that had been matured for more than twelve years. Even today, only the master blender and one or two of his colleagues have access to the original recipes, all of which remain closely guarded secrets. The name 'Walker's Kilmarnock Whisky' was dropped and replaced by the brand name 'Johnnie Walker'. New distinctive red and black labels set at a slant across a square bottle were adopted, as

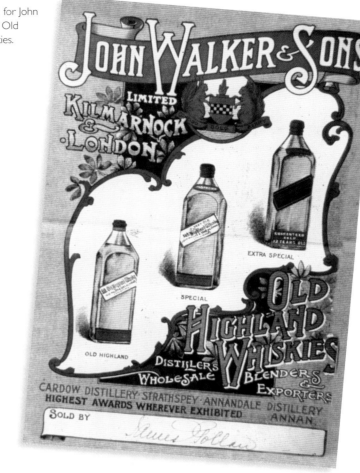

1905 sales card for John Walker & Sons Old Highland Whiskies.

was the 'Striding Man' figure trademark and the slogan 'Johnnie Walker born 1820 – still going strong'.

Registered in 1910, the Striding Man figure and slogan had come about in 1908 when it was decided to incorporate a portrait of the firm's founder into an advertising scheme. Tom Browne, a celebrated commercial artist, was commissioned to draw a cheerful Regency figure, complete with top hat, eyeglass and cane, striding out purposefully. Alongside the finished

sketch, director James Stevenson scribbled the famous slogan 'Johnnie Walker born 1820 – still going strong'. It was one of the most successful advertising promotions devised and made the name of 'Johnnie Walker' universally known. The original sketch was miraculously rescued from Walker's premises, which were bombed during the Second World War, and remains a prized possession of the company.

By 1920, Johnnie Walker was one of the three top whisky companies in the world, the others

Although registered in 1910, the 'Striding Man' and the famous slogan 'Johnnie Walker born 1820 – still going strong' featured in advertisements before then, like this one which appeared in *The Illustrated London News* in November 1909.

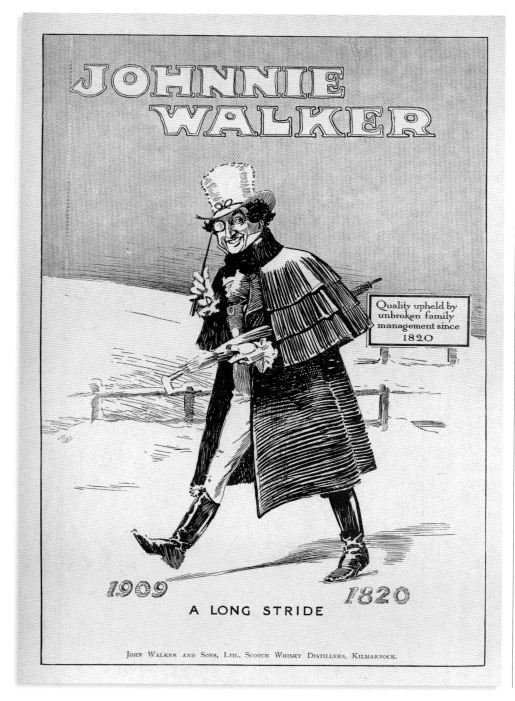

JOHNNIE WALKER

Quality upheld by unbroken family management since 1820

1909    1820

A LONG STRIDE

John Walker and Sons, Ltd., Scotch Whisky Distillers, Kilmarnock.

being Dewar and Buchanan. (Walker's went public in 1923 and in 1925 Walker, Buchanan and Dewar became part of the Distillers Company Limited.) In 1932, Johnnie Walker 'Swing' was introduced. It was uniquely packaged to appeal to transatlantic travellers and the North American market, with a curved base to the bottle that enabled it to 'swing' with a ship's movement and avoid toppling. On each crossing of the luxury transatlantic liners, over 2,500 bottles of Swing were consumed.

During the 1930s the company's progress continued, with a massive expansion of the facilities at Kilmarnock, and in 1933 Johnnie Walker was granted a royal warrant as Scotch Whisky Distillers to King George V, an honour that has been renewed by each subsequent monarch.

Shortly after the Second World War Johnnie Walker Red Label emerged as the world's leading whisky brand, and by 1955 sales had increased fivefold. As Johnnie Walker's enormous export business had brought in essential foreign currency to the war-weakened British economy, it was no surprise when in 1966 Johnnie Walker was one of the first winners of the Queen's Award for Export Achievement.

Although the famous Striding Man trademark has been used ever since it was introduced, over the years it has been modified, such as in 1999 as part of a £100 million global marketing campaign called 'Keep Walking'. Then the figure, which has always been seen walking from right to left on the bottle labels, was made to walk from left to right. This was because the

TIME MARCHES ON!

*It makes me proud to think I've seen*
*The paddle-boat become the "Queen."*
*Like Clyde-built ships, I've grown in fame*
*The skill behind me's still the same.*

JOHNNIE WALKER SCOTCH WHISKY

Born 1820 –
still going
strong

Time Marches On. An advertisement from 1948 in which Johnnie Walker says he was proud to have seen the paddle-boat become the 'Queen' – the liner *Queen Elizabeth*.

marketing men decided that the figure looked as if he was walking backwards into the past and by changing his direction he, and the whisky, were striding towards a bright future in the new millennium.

Johnnie Walker Scotch whisky (Red, Black, Gold and Blue Labels) is still blended and bottled in Kilmarnock by Diageo. As the world's best-selling Scotch whisky is Johnnie Walker Red Label, the Walker name is certainly still 'going strong'.

*Information and illustrations courtesy of Diageo.*

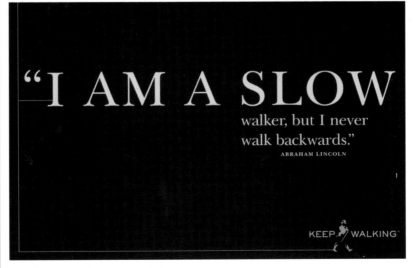

"I AM A SLOW walker, but I never walk backwards."
ABRAHAM LINCOLN

KEEP WALKING

An advert of 2001 from the global marketing campaign introduced in 1999 and called 'Keep Walking'.

# KEILLER

There is a much repeated story that husband and wife James and Janet Keiller of Dundee invented marmalade. It goes like this. Towards the end of the eighteenth century a storm-wrecked Spanish ship carrying a cargo of Seville oranges made its way into Dundee harbour. Grocer James Keiller purchased the entire cargo of oranges, but on discovering how bitter they were, he gave them to his wife, Janet, to see what she

White earthenware Keiller 'Dundee Marmalade' jar.

could do with them. Janet then invented marmalade, and she and James set up a factory to produce it.

Repeated the story may be, but it is untrue. Janet and James were mother and son, not a married couple. They had a small confectionery business where they made cakes, jams, jellies and sweets, not a grocery. There was never a whole cargo of oranges. Janet did not invent marmalade, and she and James did not set up a factory to produce it.

Marmalade had been around for a long time before Janet was said to have invented it, and although its source has been lost over the centuries, the term *marmalade* first appeared in the English language as far back as 1480. A definition given in *Chambers Cyclopedia* of 1728 defined it as a confection made of the juice or pulp of several fruits – plums, apricots, quince, etc. – boiled with sugar into a consistence. The earliest Scottish printed recipe for orange marmalade appeared in *Mrs McLintoch's Receipts of 1736*.

There is a charming tale involving Mary Queen of Scots that tells how the name marmalade

originated. Apparently, when she felt unwell Mary would have a confection of oranges made up for her, which was referred to as *Marie est malade* – hence 'Marmalade'. While the tale is charming, the word derives from the Portuguese *marmelada*, 'quince'.

Now back to the Keillers. James was the youngest son of Janet and John Keiller, a tailor. At the age of twenty-two he joined his mother in her confectionery shop on the south side of Dundee's Seagate. According to the history of Keiller's of Dundee by W. H. Mathew, which sets the record straight about the real story of the family's involvement with marmalade, James was a young man who had made 'some remarkable success in experiments with oranges'. It was he, therefore, not his mother, who produced a novel type of marmalade, based on slicing the peel and making a jelly consistency, rather than the dense and sticky substance containing peel that had been grated and beaten which had been the norm. Early marmalades had to be sliced rather than spread and were served as a dessert taken with wine and nuts

Jam-making in Keiller's factory in the early 1900s.

Britain, and when the British trademark registry was established in 1876, 'Keiller's Dundee Orange Marmalade' was one of the first trademarks registered. When Alexander died in 1877, Keiller's marmalade was being sold in Australia, New Zealand, South Africa, India and China – mainly to British expatriates.

Advertisement of 1949 which shows that, as well as manufacturing marmalades, jams, chocolates, confectionery, cakes and shortbread, Keiller had restaurants in Dundee, Perth, Montrose, Arbroath, Forfar and Blairgowrie.

rather than a breakfast conserve. It was the Scots who were the first to serve marmalade at breakfast and who took to it with hot toast and butter as a good start to the day.

James came up with his much thinner Scottish 'chip' version of marmalade in 1797, and it can only be assumed that his aptitude for innovation motivated his mother to use his name to give the company an identity. Of course, it might just have been that she was proud of her boy!

Contrary to the stories of rapid expansion into marmalade production by the Keillers, during James's working life – all of which was spent in his mother's small shop – marmalade was only a minor part of his business. Indeed, a stock-taking sheet of March 1833 shows that the firm valued their commodity holdings at £536 of which marmalade accounted for a mere £27.

After James's death, at the age of sixty-three in 1839, his widow, Margaret, and her eldest son,

Alexander, took charge of the business, and in 1840 a new shop in Castle Street was bought as well as work premises off the High Street. At that time the business was still mainly that of a confectioner but by 1850, when Alexander took control following his mother's death, marmalade-making, made easier with the introduction of peel-chopping machines and steam power, had increased and by 1867 it was the company's main product. By then Keillers had started to use the distinctive white earthenware jars that identified its 'Dundee Orange Marmalade' worldwide. The jars kept the marmalade well and helped it withstand long journeys by land and sea.

Alexander ran the company for twenty-seven years during which it ranked way above Cadbury and Rowantree. Around 1857, he opened a factory on the Channel Island of Guernsey to evade the high import duties on sugar imposed in mainland

James Keiller & Son Ltd.
Dundee

Recommend you to visit–

Keiller Restaurants
for Breakfast Coffee Lunch and Tea

at
DUNDEE · PERTH · MONTROSE
ARBROATH · FORFAR · BLAIRGOWRIE

Famous since 1797 for
Marmalades, Jams, Chocolates, Confectionery Cakes & Shortbread.

It's new **Keiller**

It's delicious

"Little Chip" Marmalade

The JELLY marmalade all children love

1951 advertisement for Keiller's new 'Little Chip' marmalade.

On Alexander's death, his son John, aged 26, took over the company, and began expanding it. He remodelled the Dundee factory, using the latest technology, and enhanced the confectionery business with a range of sweets including traditional lozenges, gums and rock. He also added chocolate products.

In 1888, by which time the sugar duties had been removed, the company switched production from Guernsey to a new factory at Silvertown in London. This was to meet the demand for Keiller's products in England and to provide a base for expansion into the export market. To this end, John Keiller travelled throughout Europe, the United States and the British colonies of Australia and New Zealand. He was not content for the company to live on its past reputation.

John Keiller controlled the company directly from 1877 to 1893 when it was converted into a limited liability company with John as chairman. Because of ill health, however, he gradually withdrew from the running of the by then hugely successful business, with a range of marmalade, jellies and jams as well as comfits, jujubes, candied peels and bottled fruits. John Keiller died in 1899, aged 49. He was the last of the Keillers to be actively involved in the business, which in 1919 merged with two English-based firms, Crosse & Blackwell and Lazenby's, with Crosse & Blackwell taking complete control in 1922.

Keiller thrived with Crosse & Blackwell and even managed to keep its head above water during the Depression when, apart from marmalade, it produced bakery goods – pies, shortbread and 200 varieties of cakes, Dundee Cake being the most popular. It was a different story, however, during the Second World War. Trade declined, and the London factory was destroyed during the Blitz. Production was then centred on the Albert Square Factory in Dundee to which the company had moved in the 1890s and which had burned down in 1900. Fire was no stranger to Keiller. It had earlier destroyed its original Dundee factory in 1860 and the London factory in 1899.

After the war, confidence returned, and Keiller modernised the Albert Square factory and built a new preserves factory at Maryfield in Dundee, which during the 1950s was extremely busy producing – as well as marmalade – lemon curd, jams, fruit squashes, cordials, mincemeat and plum puddings. Two

types of marmalade were produced – thick and clear jelly.

The start of the 1960s brought a new owner for Keiller when the Nestlé group took over Crosse and Blackwell. It also saw the boiled sweet production at the Albert Square factory increase eightfold. Despite this, however, in 1971 the factory was closed with the loss of hundreds of jobs. Meanwhile, Maryfield continued to produce marmalade, and by 1979 sales had doubled.

During the 1980s, changes of ownership of Keiller came fast and furious. Nestlé sold out to the Okhai group, which sold out to Barker & Dobson, which sold its 'Keiller Preserves' subsidiary to Rank Hovis McDougall, which quickly switched production from Maryfield to its Robertson's preserves plant in

Manchester with a promise to retain the names 'Keiller' and 'Dundee' along with the distinctive white marmalade pots.

The final nail in the coffin of the Keiller empire in Dundee came in 1992 when confectioners Alma Holdings, which had bought Barker & Dobson, went into receivership. The factory at Maryfield, where sweets such as Keiller's famous Butterscotch were produced, closed. After 195 years, the name of James Keiller & Son was no longer part of Dundee's manufacturing scene.

While Centura Foods, a division of Rank Hovis McDougall, still produce Keiller's marmalade, unfortunately it is not available in Scotland, where it started, only in Waitrose supermarkets in England and outlets abroad.

# LEES' (MACAROON BAR)

Lees' famous Macaroon Bar is firmly rooted in Scottish culture. It is one of Scotland's most popular products, requested by expatriates around the world from Canada to Australia. The delicious treat was invented by accident in 1931 when John Justice Lees, a grocer's son from Coatbridge, was trying to produce a smooth chocolate fondant bar in the premises above his father's shop in Newland Street. The result was a disaster, but as an experiment, John covered the bar in coconut and inadvertently discovered a titbit that would become a Scottish staple – the Macaroon Bar.

Other products, such as tablet, mint ice and snowballs, joined the Macaroon Bar, and by the 1950s sweet-toothed Scots could not get enough of Lees' confectionery, with Macaroon Bars becoming almost as popular on the football terraces as the half-time pies, both of which were washed down with Bovril.

Lees' products were manufactured in unusual premises, the old Garden cinema, which had been acquired by John Justice Lees. It was just 200 yards along the street from his father's shop. The stalls were the production area, the balcony the storeroom where the aisles, rows and seating numbers were ingeniously incorporated into a stock-keeping system – for example, Macaroon Bar labels might be found in row six, seat seven, except the seat was not there. The projection room was another storeroom, and the marble-stepped former ticket booths were shops where misshaped confectionery was sold.

Lees realised the power of marketing, and for their Macaroon Bars the company came up with one of the best-loved and best-remembered jingles, which was recognised everywhere long before Barr came up with its slogan 'Made

The creator of the Macaroon Bar, John Justice Lees.

in Scotland from Girders'. Generations grew up with Lees' catchy advertising song and many can still sing it now. It went as follows:

'Lees', Lees', more if you please,
All of us beg on our bended knees,
For mums and dads and
    grandpapas,
It's Lees' for luscious Macaroon
    Bars.'

Originally, there was a line about 'A tasty treat for picanninnies and grandpapas', which was swiftly changed when a subsequent generation objected to the turn of phrase.

During the 1960s and 70s Lees continued to flourish, but by the end of the1980s the glory days had come to an end and Lees' empire was crumbling. The company was still a family concern, but John Justice Lees had grown old and so had the factory. In March 1991 the company showed a loss of just under £2 million and the family was forced to sell it to Northumbrian Fine Foods. This was only a temporary reprieve, however, as despite a range of new

A Lees' production line in the old Garden cinema in the late 1960s or early 1970s.

partner, Klaus Perch-Nielsen, own over 50 per cent of Lees' equity. Other investors have 35 per cent, and 10 per cent is held by the Bank of Scotland.

Miquel, who had first arrived in Glasgow from the Channel Islands during the Second World War, had an enviable record of accomplishment. Working his way up from the shop floor, he transformed Bells from a small distillery into a worldwide brand. On arrival at Lees he said it reminded him very much of the situation Bells had been in – it was a brand that everyone in Scotland knew, loved and bought, but it had not tapped into its potential abroad and its facilities were dreadful. It did have potential, however, and it did have the Macaroon Bar.

Within a year Miquel had returned the company to

confectionery products and the development of Heather Cameron Meringues, by Christmas 1992 the company was heading for liquidation and the workers were not sure if the factory would be open when they returned after the holiday.

Fortunately, the New Year brought salvation in the form of Raymond Miquel, the former chairman of Bell's Whisky, who took control in early 1993 and returned Lees to independent Scottish ownership. Miquel and his Danish

A selection of Lees' products in the early 1970s.

Advertisement of 1971 for
Lees' Big Macaroon Bar

profitability and by 1998 had moved it to a £4.7million custom-built factory less than half a mile away from the site of the now demolished cinema and the other Heather Cameron factory. There is still a factory shop at the new site, but because of all the new machinery, there are far fewer misshapen products than in the old days when a bagful of battered snowballs, macaroon bars and tablet could be bought for a shilling.

Lees marked the tenth anniversary of its rescue from bankruptcy by acquiring another Scottish family-owned firm, Waverley Bakery Ltd, which can trace its roots back to 1908 when the Zaccerdelli and Cervi families founded Waverley Biscuits in Edinburgh. As Scotland's

only cone and wafer manufacturer, Waverley's products were complementary to Lees' products. The cone is the most environmentally friendly form of packing for ice cream, and its traditional name, 'Pokey Hat', originated from *ecco un poco* (Italian for 'try a little'), the phrase used by Italian ice-cream street vendors when peddling their wares. Wafers first appeared in Europe around the 1660s. Incidentally, Britain has the third highest consumption of ice cream in Europe per head, at around 8 litres per year, far out-weighing Italy's consumption, which is only about 3.5 litres. Vanilla flavour accounts for 90 per cent of sales.

Over 50 million Lees' Snowballs are sold in the UK market each year, and if they were put end-to-end, they would stretch from Glasgow to Paris and back.

Apart from producing its renowned Macaroon Bars, Snowballs and Teacakes, Lees is the UK's biggest manufacturer of meringues. It produces over 200,000 meringues nests per day and has 85 per cent of

all retail sales. Newer products are Snowcakes, Jaffa Delights and a Dennis the Menace Bar. Lees struck a licensing deal with D. C. Thomson to use *The Beano*'s Dennis the Menace character on a Coconut'n'Ice bar, Lees' first product aimed specifically at children. Originally, Miquel had wanted to license Oor Wullie, another of Thomson's best-loved creations, but Thomson stuck to its long-standing policy of not licensing either Oor Wullie or the Broons.

With its products available from corner shops to major multiples, Lees has again established itself as a nation's favourite. It also exports worldwide, with even the King of Tonga being a fan of its Macaroon Bars, having been introduced to them by expatriate Scots.

Things look good for the future, so, as the jingle goes:
'Lees', Lees', more if you please'.

*Illustrations courtesy of Lees.*

The ever popular Lees' Snowballs.

# LYLE'S GOLDEN SYRUP

Lyle's Golden Syrup has been named by the *Guinness Book of Records* as Britain's oldest brand. Its story began in the 1860s when Abram Lyle III became involved with the Glebe Sugar Refinery in Greenock.

Lyle was born in 1820 in Greenock, and worked as a cooper (barrel maker) in his father's business, before starting a small shipping business. He had been transporting sugar for years, when, as payment of a debt, he took a part-share in a local sugar refinery. Discovering that the sugar cane refining process produced a syrup that normally went to waste, he decided to experiment with this by-product and discovered a process that produced a delicious sweet spread and sweetener for cooking.

Wanting a purely family business, Abram sold his shares in the Glebe Refinery and sent his sons Abram IV and Charles Lyle, who had been managing the Glebe Refinery, to London to look for a site for the family's own refinery. Land was bought in Plaistow marshes in Silvertown, and in 1882 the Plaistow Sugar Refinery was completed. Many of the workers were brought from Greenock with their families.

In the first year, 1883, the venture made a loss of £30,000, but demand was growing for the golden liquid Lyle stored in wooden casks and sold to his staff and locals, and soon it was being delivered to shops in casks, decanted into dispensers and then poured out into customers' own jars. About a tonne a week was being sold, and a

Abram Lyle

separate part of the refinery was devoted to the product.

In 1885 the product was poured into tins for the first time. Although the style of the tin has altered little over the years, during the First World War the container was made from stiff cardboard instead of tin that was needed for the war effort.

The tins were strong, and explorer Captain Scott took some on his ill-fated Antarctic expedition in 1910. When explorers discovered some of the tins in 1956 both the tin and syrup inside it were in good condition.

It was Abram who designed the product's packaging that today is instantly recognisable by 86 percent of shoppers. He was a religious man, which is why the Lyle's Golden Syrup trademark depicts a quotation from the Bible. The Old Testament *Book of Judges*, Chapter 14, tells the story of Samson slaying the lion and later finding a swarm of bees forming a comb of honey in the carcass. Samson made this the subject of a riddle: 'Out of the eater came forth meat and out of the strong came forth sweetness'.

LYLE'S GOLDEN SYRUP

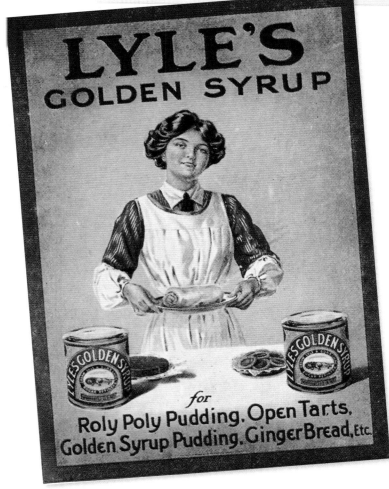

Above. Well-known
Boy and Girl
Showcard c. 1900s.

Left. Lady Cooking
Showcard c. 1910s.

Abram decided to have the dead lion and the bees and the second half of the quotation put on all his tins, and in 1904 the lion, bees and quotation were registered as Lyle's trademark. The famous design has since been recognised by the *Guinness Book of World Records* as the world's oldest brand.

By the beginning of the 20th century, Lyle's Golden Syrup was an institution and George V gave it a royal warrant.

In 1921 the business merged with Tate, a sugar-refining business started by Henry Tate in 1859. The merger produced Tate & Lyle, today the only cane sugar refiner in the UK and the largest in Europe. A rule of the merger, however, was that the Golden Syrup could only be produced at Plaistow.

Throughout the Second World War, the factory operated round-the-clock shifts, 2000 people being employed there. Situated in the East End, however, the factory was a target for the Luftwaffe. At one point, it suffered air raids for 69 consecutive days and 79 consecutive nights, but despite being hit by six high-explosive bombs, 61 incendiary bombs and one parachute mine, only one member of staff was killed on duty. As workers' homes were bombed, the company built reinforced dormitories and even installed a full-time hairdresser to boost its workers' morale.

The Three Ways House Hotel in the Cotswolds has a 'Syrup Sponge Room' inspired by Lyle's Golden Syrup. The bed has been created to look like a sponge pudding with syrup drizzling from it and the room is adorned with Lyle's Golden Syrup paraphernalia, even a

Showcard c. 1935
Every Dog Has
Its Day.

Selection of McVitie & Price biscuits for Christmas 1950.

opened in 1886. Concurrently the name of the firm was changed to take account of the constant use in Glasgow of the founder's name and was from then on known as Macfarlane Lang & Co. (The Victoria Biscuit Works was transferred to a new site at Tollcross in 1925, and is the site of the present McVitie biscuit operation in Glasgow.) A proud boast of Macfarlane Lang was that Queen Victoria always had a tin of its Parmena biscuits on her luncheon table. It also produced Granola Digestive biscuits, the rival of McVitie's Digestives. Other famous biscuits were Gypsy Creams and Chocolate Viennas.

After the formation of United Biscuits under the chairmanship of Peter MacDonald, McVitie's legal adviser since the 1930s, both Macfarlane Lang and McVitie & Price retained their separate identities and competed against each other, McVitie developing market dominance, particularly in Digestive, Rich Tea and Homewheat. It also began producing today's popular Jaffa Cakes with their 'smashing orangey bit in the middle'. It was not only the two companies who competed against each other, however – the three McVitie factories at Edinburgh, Manchester and London were being conducted independently, even to the extent of having different recipes for the same kind of biscuit. Obviously, something had to be done, but it was not until 1965 that the operations of the two companies were integrated into a single company with Hector Laing, son-in-law of Alexander Grant, as managing director.

By 1965 two other Scottish bakeries had joined United Biscuits – Crawfords and Macdonalds.

opening a small shop and bakery in Gallowgate, Glasgow, then one of the principal business streets. James Lang's nephew, who took over the business on his uncle's death in 1841, expanded the firm and when he brought in his two sons in 1878 named it John Macfarlane & Sons. The name of Lang stuck to the business, however, and as long as

bread was made it was known throughout Glasgow and the surrounding district as 'Lang's Breid'. At that time only a few hand-made biscuits were produced.

In 1884 the firm decided to move into biscuit manufacturing, and on a site adjoining the bread factory in Wesleyan Street, it built the Victoria Biscuit Works, which

Advertisement in *Punch* magazine of December 1954 for Crawford's shortbread, which shows how long it took for production of such fare to return to normal after the Second World War. Note the small earlier advertisement in the left-hand corner of the picture which states that 'Christmas waits, and so must we for Crawford Tartan Shortbread'.

Crawfords, which claimed to be the 'Oldest of Biscuit Manufacturers', began in 1813 when William Crawford opened a small bakery shop in Leith, the port for Edinburgh. By 1860 William's son, with the help of his own sons (he had eight, five of whom followed him into the business) had expanded the small bakery into a well-known and well-patronised business about to go into factory-scale production in Elbe Street, Leith. In 1897 production capacity was expanded by the opening of a factory in Liverpool. Between them, the two factories produced over thirteen million biscuits in every working day throughout the year.

Shortbread was a national delicacy in Scotland, but the thick biscuits did not appeal in England. Crawfords' solution was to make thinner shortbread in Liverpool, and when 'assorted' shortbread in round tins was introduced in 1910/11, it was a runaway success. The salesmen sold it enthusiastically, one of them so successfully that he was known as the 'Shortbread King'. Apart from turning shortbread into a national taste, Crawfords pioneered products such as Butter Puffs.

With a splendid record of family tradition and a highly successful century and a half of expansion, in 1962 Crawford joined

McVitie & Price and Macfarlane Lang by becoming part of United Biscuits.

The fourth Scottish biscuit company to join United Biscuits was Macdonalds, founded in Glasgow by William Macdonald who began his business life as a salesman. Working in turn for several biscuit manufacturers, each move he made was upwards financially until, as Scottish sales manager on a commission basis for a prominent biscuit company, his earnings were so substantial that the directors wanted to cut his commission. William declined the suggestion and decided to work for himself, and in 1925 he

set up as a food commission agent.

With his reputation as an outstanding salesman, William soon had several well-known confectionery manufacturers as clients. He also imported large quantities of cream-filled wafers from Antwerp, which he sold at less than half the price of similar products on the market. He then leased a former ordnance factory in Cardonald, Glasgow, and began chocolate-coating biscuits manufactured by others. This was successful, and in 1928 he became a biscuit manufacturer, a brave decision, as he was fifty-three years of age and had a

# Home sweet Homewheat

McVITIE'S HOMEWHEAT: THE ONLY ONE WITH THAT PERFECT COMBINATION
OF CRUMBLY DIGESTIVE BISCUIT AND THICK RICH CHOCOLATE, MILK OR PLAIN.

Colourful and creative Homewheat advertisement of 1979.

the recipe used British wheat while competitors imported theirs. Homewheat was McVitie's first chocolate-coated product. If all the Homewheat biscuits eaten in one year were put side by side, they would stretch around the world more than twice.

In 1986 Hobnobs, an oaty-textured biscuit with a home-baked appearance and taste, arrived. The name came from 'hob', as in ovens, and 'nob', as in a nob of butter. The brand, now in various forms, went from strength to strength, with sales quickly growing but not affecting existing brands.

Recognising that fat was now a national concern, the reduced-fat Go Ahead! range was devised in 1996 to provide a snack that could be included as part of a nourishing and balanced diet. A series of TV ads fronted by fitness guru 'Mr Motivator' promoted the brand as a 'better for you' alternative to mainstream snacks. Each commercial had the catchphrase 'Go Ahead! Make your day'. The range is now one of the UK's top ten biscuit brands.

Because of the longevity of the brand, its reputation for quality and its ability to keep up with contemporary consumer trends, McVitie's is sure to delight the palates of biscuit-lovers for many more years.

wife and six children to support. William sold his range at one shilling (5p) per pound. Competitors' products sold at 1/4d. (7p) per pound. Quality was paramount. Butter was the only fat William Macdonald allowed to be used.

After the Second World War Macdonalds produced only two biscuits – Glengarry, a round shortcake biscuit, and Penguin, a chocolate-covered oblong cream biscuit. This continued until 1950 when Munchmallow was launched, followed by Yoyo, Bandit and Taxi. In

1964 Macdonalds Biscuits became part of United Biscuits, the merger giving United Biscuits a dominant market share in chocolate count lines.

After the formation of United Biscuits, McVitie & Price, or McVitie's as the brand is now known, steadily increased its share of the market and although new products have been introduced, Digestive and Homewheat Chocolate Digestive have remained as the core products. Homewheat began life in the early 1900s and gained its name because

® Bandit, Crawford's Go Ahead!, Hobnobs, Homewheat, MacVita, McVitie's, Jaffa Cakes, Munchmallow, Penguin, Taxi and YoYo, are registered trademarks of United Biscuits (UK) Limited and used by consent.

# MACKIE'S OF SCOTLAND

While Mackie's ice cream is the brand leader in the luxury ice cream market in Scotland as well as having an increasing market share in England, British visitors to South Korea must be surprised to find ice cream/café parlours going by the name of Mackie's. This exciting venture began with a London store visit by Kyung Wood Kim, Director of M & B Korea Co Ltd, when he selected Mackie's Traditional Ice Cream as his favourite from the full available range of UK ice creams.

Shipping to Seoul began in 2002 with the supply of ice cream for the Korean World Cup games. Each shipment has to spend about 36 days at sea on a journey of over 11,000 nautical miles, followed by a final train journey to Seoul. Temperature is tracked throughout the voyage.

Korea has the highest population density in the world, and with 50% of the population living in the Seoul metropolitan area, there is a well-established market for ice cream in which Mackie's aim is to become one of the country's top three ice cream brands.

M & B Korea Co Ltd has been rebranded as Mackie's of Asia, and their intention is to expand by franchise in South Korea and from there throughout Asia and possibly Japan.

Back home, Mackie's of Scotland is a family business, and since the start of the 20th century four generations have farmed at Westertown Farm near Inverurie in the North East of Scotland.

In 1986 the direction of the

A Mackie's Ice Cream Parlour in Seoul.

The Mackie family with Elgin Allie, one of the farm's Jersey cows that produce the creamiest milk. From left to right, the family members are: Halldis Mackie, Mac Mackie, Karin Hayhow, Kirsten Mackie and Maitland Mackie.

On the farm, the welfare of the cows is paramount, for they produce the most important ingredients of fresh milk and cream. A happy cow also produces more milk, so each cow has a bed area complete with a mattress in the parlour. They have feed available at all times, with fresh food added twice a day, and the vet comes on a routine visit once a week. Jersey cows were selected because they produce the creamiest milk, about 20 litres each day, which is equivalent to about 2.5 litres of double cream. To produce this amount of cream, the cows each eat 35kg of food every day and deposit 50 litres of muck! Mackie's collection of 9 milking robots is the largest voluntary access milking centre in

business changed, with a shift from traditional farming and milk retail into ice cream production, a transition completed in 1993 when the family converted the traditional byre and old mill into a modern ice cream dairy that can produce over 10 million litres of ice cream each year. A New Product Development kitchen was also created.

Although the most popular product in Mackie's range is 'Traditional', a smooth, creamy ice cream with no added flavours, new products, such as Strawberry and Raspberry Dairy Sorbets and Mango and Orange Iced Fruit Smoothies, have also won excellence and innovation awards.

The farming activity covers 1600 acres of land, and the herd of 500 Jersey and Holstein milking cows are the main focus of the farm, utilising most of the land on which is grown 600 acres of grass and 900 acres of cereal, the bulk of which is processed into feed for the cattle

Mackie's Traditional Ice Cream, the company's first and most popular product.

Mackie's mouth-watering fruit smoothies.

Europe. The process from milking to ice cream can be completed in less than 24 hours.

Managing the environment is important to Mackie's, who have planted 120 acres of deciduous trees around the farm for beauty and to provide wildlife habitats. Environmental corridors, a wetland area and pond have also been created to protect and encourage as diverse a wildlife population as possible. The company commitment to the environment is displayed by three 750KW wind turbines which generate all the electricity required for the business – with enough surplus to power about 1000 domestic homes. Mackie's ice cream is made with renewable energy, and

in 2008 a new form of packaging will be launched because it is lighter and more easily recyclable.

In 2007 Mackie's was the regional winner for Europe, Middle East and Africa, of the *Financial Times* Environmental Awards, and the company's vision is to be 'a global brand from the greenest company in Britain created by people having fun'.

### SOME FACTS ABOUT ICE CREAM

● Ice cream was invented in China around 200 BC, when a soft milk and rice mixture was solidified by packing it in snow.
● The first documented evidence of ice cream in England was in 1672 during the reign of Charles II. At the Feast of St George in 1671 the only

table to be served ices was the king's, with one plate of white strawberries and one plate of ice cream.
● First class passengers on the Titanic were treated to French ice cream for dessert according to a menu of 14 April 1912. Second class passengers had to make do with plain egg-free American ice cream.
● Immigrants to America, arriving in Ellis Island in the 1920s, were given ice cream as part of the introduction to a typical American menu. Some arrivals mistakenly spread this 'frozen butter' on their bread.

Infomation and illustrations courtesy of Mackie's

# MARSHALLS' MACARONI

Marshalls is the leading pasta brand in Scotland. It is produced and marketed by Pasta Foods Ltd, a world leader in the production and marketing of 'snack pellets' and the UK's leading dry pasta producer. The traditional Marshalls brand, however, has been part of the Scottish menu for generations as it goes back to 1878 when James Marshall, the pioneer of pre-packed refined wheat-based foodstuffs, set up the Ibrox Flour Mills in Glasgow's south side.

Marshall was born in Rothesay in 1838 and moved to Glasgow in his early twenties to work in W. & W. Glen's flour mill in Cheapside Street. Although he became a partner in Glens in 1865, Marshall wanted to work for himself and established his own flour mill producing farinaceous substances known as 'Marshalls' Preparations of Wheat'. Testimony by the medical profession and analyses by chemists that these preparations 'contained all the elements necessary for the sustenance and growth of the human frame' gained them the confidence of the public.

Marshalls' first branded product was Semolina, which contained all the elements of the wheat grain without the inclusion of any crude or indigestible products. Cheaper than bread, it was just as nutritious. *The Lancet* medical journal wrote of it: 'Marshalls' Semolina is entirely satisfactory. Analysis proves that it is absolutely free from adulteration. We regard it as a highly valuable form of food.' All that was required to make semolina the perfect food was the addition of a little fat, which is why it was always cooked with milk or with a little bit of butter. It was much more digestible than oatmeal.

Apart from medical endorsements, there were lighter

Trademark 'Heart of the Wheat'.

promotions for Semolina such as poems extolling its virtue. The following are verses from one of these:

I used to think that Scotch Oatmeal
Was guid enough for ony chiel;
But I hae changed my mind gey
    weel
Since tasting Semolina.
Ma wife, she cooks it every day
Wi' milk and eggs, frae June till May;
There's naething better, she daurs
    say
Than Marshall's Semolina.
We're free frae care, my wife an' me,
An' happy wi' our bairnies three,
An we've never paid a doctor's fee
Since using Semolina.

Marshalls' Semolina was introduced in 1885, and although James Marshall was not the first to manufacture it, his was different in that it was pre-packed, the first such product to become available on the market and an innovation that gained his company a lasting reputation. In the same year Marshalls' products were protected by the trademark 'The Heart of the Wheat' and James's brother, Thomas, an engineer and an

Advertisement of 1893 for Farola.

active food reformer, became a partner in the business.

Together, James and Thomas launched Marshalls' second branded product, Farola, a very fine-grained semolina advertised as 'pleasing to the most fastidious and easily digested by the most delicate'. It was marketed as having many uses: mixed with fruit to make blancmanges and other 'ornamental table dishes', as an infant food, an invalid food and as a health food. 'Farola is beautifully clear. The microscope shows it is pure wheat,' said *The Lancet*. Other medical journals also proclaimed its purity, such endorsements forming the basis of the company's advertising. Registered in 1885, the name Farola came from the Latin *far* – 'corn' – with the fashionable Victorian ending 'ola' (as in 'pianola').

In recognition of their superior quality and excellence, Marshalls' Farola and Semolina received gold medals at the Edinburgh and Liverpool Exhibitions in 1886.

The partnership between the Marshall brothers did not last for long. High marketing costs and an over-ambitious level of production forced it into liquidation in 1887. When sales of £11,000 were offset against the cost of raw materials, operating costs and advertising, there was a shortfall of nearly £2,000 and without the resources to sustain such a loss and creditors pressing for payment, James Marshall chose sequestration.

There then followed an acrimonious dispute between the brothers that led to the business being reconstructed into two companies, James continuing at the

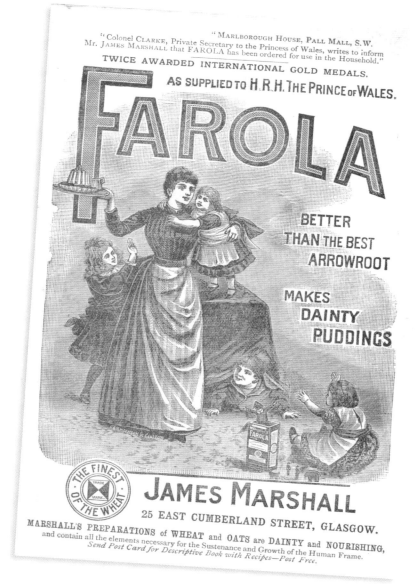

"MARLBOROUGH HOUSE, PALL MALL, S.W.
"Colonel CLARKE, Private Secretary to the Princess of Wales, writes to inform
Mr. JAMES MARSHALL that FAROLA has been ordered for use in the Household."

TWICE AWARDED INTERNATIONAL GOLD MEDALS.

AS SUPPLIED TO H.R.H. THE PRINCE OF WALES.

# FAROLA

BETTER THAN THE BEST ARROWROOT

MAKES DAINTY PUDDINGS

THE FINEST OF THE WHEAT

# JAMES MARSHALL
25 EAST CUMBERLAND STREET, GLASGOW.

MARSHALL'S PREPARATIONS of WHEAT and OATS are DAINTY and NOURISHING, and contain all the elements necessary for the Sustenance and Growth of the Human Frame. Send Post Card for Descriptive Book with Recipes—Post Free.

Ibrox Mill and Thomas setting up in Morrison Street. There was war as each brother battled to capture the market. Thomas claimed to have retained the old firm's trademark, 'The Heart of the Wheat', and warned customers that 'without it none are genuine'. Under the mark he sold semolina and oat flour. On the other hand, James retained the old firm's brand names and advertised himself as sole proprietor

of Semolina and Farola.

To gain supremacy, each brother brought out new products. James created Tritola, a large-grained, fine-quality semolina, and Ptyaloid, a pure vegetable digestant of starch, highly recommended by physicians for cases of 'weak digestion or debility'. He also produced Granola, a wholemeal semolina manufactured for those requiring a diet containing all the parts of the wheat. Its

granular form made it convenient for use in puddings and porridge and for mixing with soft flour to make bread, scones and biscuits. Thomas introduced Kassama Food, 'a delicate nourishing preparation got wholly from wheat', which was claimed to have 'obtained an almost worldwide celebrity'.

Although James Marshall had the branded products, he found life difficult in the early years of the reconstruction. Nevertheless, he persevered and in 1888 opened a new packing plant and office in the east end of Glasgow and a small warehouse in London's Pimlico. A year later, he obtained official patents for Marshalls' Semolina and Farola and the trademark 'The Finest of the Wheat'.

Although some of the problems of direct competition were eased with the closure of his brother's firm in 1894, following his death the previous year, it was imperative for James Marshall to

keep his company's name to the forefront. This he did by advertising extensively in newspapers and magazines and on billboards. He also came to an agreement with bakers Macfarlane Lang (for whom his son,

James P. Marshall, was a bakery manager) allowing them to use the trademarks Granola and Farola for biscuits based on the products. Later, Marshall sold Macfarlane Lang the sole right to the title Granola and, in exchange, Macfarlane Lang reconveyed to Marshalls the right to use Farola for biscuits.

In 1900 James Marshall converted his firm into a private limited company with the shares distributed among his family. James Marshall and his son James, still employed by Macfarlane Lang, were the only directors until 1906 when two of James' other sons, Thomas and Allan, joined the board. Three years later, his fourth son, Edward, became a director at the age of eighteen.

In the period leading up to the First World War there was little change to the product range. Progress was made in establishing an export market, largely with British colonies, particularly Kenya. During

A page from the 'Nursery Rhymes Up to Date' booklet showing Little Bo Beep. Note that there was space left to insert the product's name in the picture. The poetry left much to be desired.

the war, production was switched to provisioning the British Army, and while home markets were quickly re-established after the war, exports, which had been around 41 tons in 1914, shrank to single figures. While the company survived the war, Allan Marshall was killed, a great blow to his father who was eighty at the time. From 1919 onwards James Marshall became increasingly blind, and in 1926 he suffered a further tragedy when his son Thomas died from pneumonia.

During the 1920s, with James Marshall still at the helm (he found it hard to delegate), the company continued to increase sales by creative advertising. It missed very few trade fairs and exhibitions, undertook market research, produced recipe books and provided a variety of special offers such as calendars and tea trays. According to the company's archives, one woman who received a tea tray complained about the advertisement on its upperside and said that she did not like to use it when she had guests. She suggested that the advertisement should have been on the underside as some other companies had done.

Although the company produced an average of 980 tons of Semolina and Farola a year, the Scottish market, particularly Glasgow, dominated sales. Other areas of consequence were the northeast of England and, in Ireland, Belfast and Dublin.

On 28 May 1928 James Marshall died of heart failure. He had been dedicated to the business and, apart from taking a short break when his son Thomas died, he played an active role until the day before his death.

Advertisement of 1946 featuring Marshalls' three branded products – Farola, Macaroni and Semolina. Their Scottishness was emphasised by framing the picture with tartan. The wording of the advert shows that supplies were available only in limited quantities because of the Second World War.

In 1935 the company introduced the third of its famous branded products, Marshalls' Macaroni. Manufacturers had pursued the idea of producing pasta products before the war but had failed because of difficulties in perfecting the drying process. These had been overcome by the late 1920s and a variety of pasta products, largely unknown to the British table, were introduced. Marshalls was the first in Scotland to start manufacturing macaroni products on a commercial basis and advertised itself as the firm that put the 'Mac in Macaroni'.

While pasta products were being introduced, production of Farola and Semolina continued and, according to letters in the company's archives, they were very well thought of. One lady wrote that she had received a packet of Farola in a parcel sent to her in 1947. Over the next year she used the Farola to make shortbread biscuits and, on coming to the end of it, she found an advertising card relating to the Empire Exhibition in 1938. The Farola was ten years old and must have been stored through the war years. It was in perfect condition.

Over the decades since, James Marshall has expanded into making just about every kind of pasta imaginable, and although the company's ownership has changed, the quality of its products has not. As in the past, great attention is paid to packaging and today a traditional tartan band across the top of a see-through packet that displays the pasta shapes distinguishes Marshalls' products from others. The range includes Macaroni, Spaghetti, Lasagne, Tagliatelle and, of course, the company's famous Semolina and Farola, both of which have stood the test of time.

# MOTHERS PRIDE

Bread is Scotland's healthiest fast food and offers exceptionally good value for money – penny for penny it contains more nutrients than any other food. It can help provide a healthy balanced diet for everyone. When it comes to which is the most popular kind of bread, however, plain is very much an integral part of the Scottish culture. Ask any Scot what reminds him or her of Scotland and plain bread will be one of the answers. Ask which brand is preferred and it's probable the answer will be Mothers Pride whose distinctive tartan paper wrapper makes it instantly recognisable on the supermarket shelves.

Part of British Bakeries, Mothers Pride has a bakery in Glasgow, a distribution depot in Motherwell and over 700 employees in Scotland. The bakery in Glasgow produces around a quarter of a million loaves per day, 80,000 of which are plain bread.

Mothers Pride plain bread has been around since 1958, and until the 1970s plain bread was a bigger-selling loaf than pan bread. (Pan bread is so called because it is baked in a 'pan', or a tin.) Plain bread is sometimes called 'square' bread. Its dimensions are three and a half inches by seven inches, and it used to be baked in batches of two, thus a square. The main difference between a pan loaf and a Scottish plain loaf is the way the latter is produced. It is not baked in tins but on a travelling sole oven, which is effectively baked on a hot plate and batched across the oven. This gives it a hard crust on the top and bottom and soft crumb on the sides. The product is set off on a travelling wood frame that not only assists in batching of the product but also gives it a slightly woody aroma and

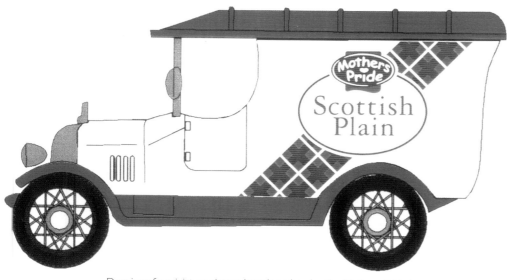

Drawing of a miniature vintage bread van bearing the Mothers Pride logo. In 2003, 4,000 of these vans were donated by Mothers Pride to raise money for the Children's Hospice Association Scotland (CHAS)

taste. To give the product stability, Scottish plain also uses stronger flour than normal white breads. Mothers Pride Scottish Plain is baked with flour milled in Scotland and has 15 per cent more protein than 'normal' white bread.

Scottish plain is made by a very traditional process compared to pan bread, which is now highly automated. Plain bread is also baked very slowly for around one and a half hours as opposed to pan bread, which is baked for around twenty minutes. Scottish plain is wrapped in a wax-paper wrapper, the traditional bread wrapping.

When it comes to making toast, research conducted by Mothers Pride found that consumers felt Scottish plain toast was far superior to other white breads. It doesn't go soggy when spread with butter or served as beans on toast. It doesn't fall apart when dunked in soup and makes great 'soldiers' for dipping into soft-boiled eggs. Toast is not the only way in which the product is consumed. When it is fresh, consumers will almost binge on it. In addition, a 'jeely piece' is not a true jam sandwich unless it's made with plain bread.

Plain bread is much more popular on the west coast of Scotland. Mothers Pride Scottish Plain is generally not distributed farther south than Newcastle upon Tyne. It does, however, make its way down in small quantities and can sometimes be found in larger Tesco, Somerfield, and Co-op stores. Sales in the south tend to be concentrated where there is strong representation of Scottish exiles, such as in Corby, Northamptonshire.

*Information and illustrations courtesy of Mothers Pride.*

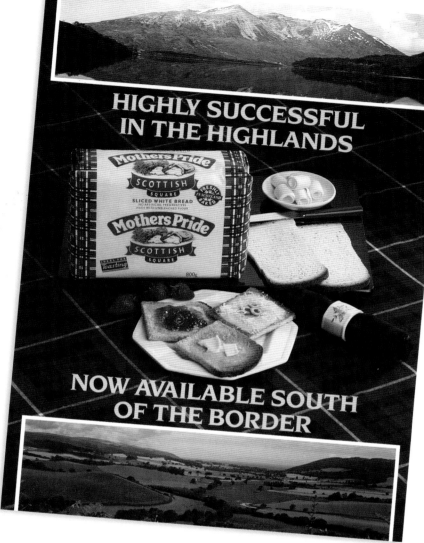

A 1989 promotional card that indicated that Mothers Pride Scottish Square Bread was now available south of the border.

### SOME FACTS ABOUT BREAD
- Our preference for white bread goes back further than we might think. In the Middle Ages, aristocrats banned the poor from eating white bread, insisting that the rougher brown was ideal for satisfying manual workers but caused wind in those with more inactive lives.
- The phrase 'upper crust' originated because the rich kept the best bits of the loaves, leaving the blackened base of the bread for everyone else.
- During the Second World War, heavy brown bread was introduced as the 'national loaf'.
- After the war sliced bread made an appearance.

Despite the availability of various kinds of bread, sliced white claims 70 per cent of the market.

# PAROZONE

For such an old and prominent brand as Parozone, the only information available about its beginnings is that contained in an advertisement of 1931:

**A Famous Glasgow Product that Keeps British Homes Clean**

Just over forty years ago, in 1891, Dr E. J. Mills, an eminent chemist of the Royal Technical College, Glasgow, made a discovery of more than ordinary interest to housewives.

This was a special secret formula for a powerful but safe household cleanser and bleach, which was to bring Science to the wash-tub, lighten labour in the home and save time in countless daily tasks.

This epoch-making discovery revolutionised domestic washing and house cleaning in Scotland and Scottish housewives were quick to welcome a new and valuable friend in Parozone.

Since then, the advance of Parozone has been sure and steady, until now, in 1931, it is used throughout the United Kingdom by all home-proud housewives who esteem purity and cleanliness.

It is pleasing to note that despite this great expansion, Glasgow remains the headquarters of the Parozone Co. Ltd., and the distinctly Scottish character of the firm continues unchanged.

Advertisements for household cleaners in the 1930s had a touch of emotional blackmail about them. Manufacturers linked doing the family wash with upholding family values. Housewives who took a pride in producing bright, clean clothing and clean homes were indicating that they took good care of their families. To have lesser standards was to be guilty of slovenly behaviour and of showing a lack of maternal responsibility. Advertisements also appealed to housewives' economical side by stating that products such as Parozone did away with all boiling and scrubbing, which meant that clothes lasted longer. It is believed that the name 'Parozone' was intended to have connotations of good health and cleanliness, with the two elements of the name, 'par ozone', suggesting a meaning of 'by the sea' – the sea and bleach having a common link in chlorine.

The distinctly Scottish character of the firm mentioned in the 1931 advertisement continued until 1963 when Jeyes acquired the product, at that time a thin solution of sodium hypochlorite bleach sold in glass bottles and used mainly for laundry. With the introduction of thickened bleaches in the 1970s, however, coupled with improved laundry powders becoming available, liquid bleach usage moved away from laundry and the main use became toilet-cleaning.

Under the Jeyes banner the Parozone brand became a market leader with many UK firsts. Among them were: perfumed bleach; a 'flip-top' cap with a liftable nozzle, making the bleach easier to direct under the toilet rim; liquid bleach with added limescale deterrent; a 'drop-in' cistern bleach block; flushable toilet surface wipes; and a liquid rim product to deliver bleach and fragrance.

Glasgow's Dr Mills would be gratified to know that his Parozone lives on, although much removed from his pioneering product.

'You don't know how white, white can be until you use Parozone!' Advertisement of 1936.

'Home is Brighter the Parozone Way'. Advertisement of 1952.

# PENGUIN BISCUITS

Although Penguin chocolate biscuits now come under the McVitie banner, it is such a popular brand that it deserves a mention of its own. It was not originally a McVitie product. It was created in 1932 by Macdonalds Biscuits, founded in Glasgow by William Macdonald who began his business life as a salesman working for several biscuit manufacturers. He then went out on his own as a food commission agent and as a side-line imported cream-filled wafers from Antwerp which he sold at less than half the price of similar products on the market. Next he leased a small factory in Cardonald, Glasgow, and began chocolate-coating biscuits manufactured by others, which was so successful that in 1928 he became a biscuit manufacturer, a cherished ambition and a brave decision, as he was fifty-three years old and had a wife and six children to support.

It is not known why the name 'Penguin' and the symbol of a giant emperor penguin was chosen by William Macdonald and his advertising agents, but whatever the reason the name has become one of the most well-known and popular in the history of chocolate biscuits.

After William Macdonald Biscuits joined United Biscuits in 1964, the brand came under the McVitie banner. (McVitie and Macfarlane Lang had formed United Biscuits in 1948.) Over the years, McVitie's association with the appealing birds, represented in Penguin advertising, has strengthened the brand. The name is regarded as memorable and fun, and has led to such entertaining advertising campaigns as 'P-P-P-Pick up a Penguin', with which McVitie's introduced Penguins on television in 1965 with the actor Derek Nimmo saying the memorable words.

Pick up a Penguin is exactly what Russian Premier Vladimir Putin did in 1991 when he was a bodyguard for Anatoly Sobchak, Mayor of Leningrad. They were part of a trade delegation to Ford's Bakery in Prestonpans, East Lothian,

Wrapper for Penguin Chukka.

and were there to close a deal to set up a bakery in Leningrad to train Russian bakers how to make biscuits. Apparently, at the signing ceremony, Putin, having spotted a plate of Penguin biscuits on the table, went over, picked up a handful and stuffed them into a pocket. As he left, everyone could see the biscuits sticking out of his pocket.

'Perfect when you're Peckish'. Along with other chocolate biscuit bars, Penguin benefits from the increasing number of people needing tasty, satisfying biscuits that can be eaten 'on the hoof' or as part of a packed lunch.

Autumn 1995 saw the introduction of the first new Penguin flavour since the original milk chocolate version. It was 'Penguin in the Dark', a darker chocolate biscuit covered with dark chocolate. McVitie's used a unique recipe with all the taste of dark chocolate without the bitterness associated with it. This successful venture led to the introduction of the Penguin Variety – a multi-pack of milk, plain, orange and mint chocolate biscuit bars.

The start of the twenty-first century saw a relaunch of the brand and new Penguin products such as Splatz – vanilla- or chocolate-flavour cream splatted between two chocolate biscuits. Also new was Chukka – flip-top pots filled with biscuit, chocolate and caramel pieces. Chukka was introduced with a fun TV advertising campaign featuring three Highlanders dressed in kilts and tossing cabers. They run out of cabers and just as they are wondering where to get more, a happy-go lucky penguin carrying a fishing rod comes along and says 'Hello, Ladies, seen any wild trout

According to this advert from 1952, there was nothing like a Penguin. Covered with creamiest milk chocolate it was only 3$\frac{1}{2}$d. for the biggest chocolate treat. Customers were invited to look for the bright red, green or blue foil wrappers when they were shopping. 'Have a Penguin today' it finished.

about?' The men look at each other and the penguin becomes a caber and gets 'Chukked'. Penguin is McVitie's most popular chocolate biscuit bar, with sales growing daily.

# PRINGLE

Although Pringle Scotland is an internationally renowned quality fashion brand, for over a hundred years underwear was its mainstay.

Pringle, one of the oldest names in the Scottish Borders, the birthplace of Scotland's knitwear industry, was founded in Hawick in 1815 by Robert Pringle. Initially it produced woollen hosiery but by 1827 was manufacturing men's and women's knitted underwear, using the highest-quality wool fibres.

Business increased, and in 1858 Pringle was the first company in Hawick to introduce the steam-driven frame. It was also when Robert's son, Walter, invented intarsia knitting, such as its diamond pattern for which Pringle became famous. Robert died in 1859, and Walter carried on Robert Pringle & Son, which in 1868 moved to larger premises by the River Teviot in Walter's Wynd, its third factory location and nicknamed Rodono after Robert Pringle's shooting lodge at St Mary's Loch.

In 1878, at the age of sixteen, Walter's son, Robert, joined the company as an apprentice, indentured for the traditional four years. He began with a salary of five shillings a week in the first year, which rose to twelve shillings a week in the fourth year. By the time Robert finished his apprenticeship the company was exporting to wholesale warehouses in the United States and Canada, so he was sent to America in 1884 to gain experience in these markets. A year later, he became a partner in the company.

During the last decade of the nineteenth century Pringle was a pioneer in the underwear world. It introduced spun-silk underwear, which became a world-famous brand. (This led to Pringle becoming known as the 'Silk House of Hawick'.) A method of using silk thread and wool thread with all the silk showing on one side was invented and patented. Underwear topped with knitted lace was introduced, as were seamless gores

A selection of Pringle women's underwear dating from 1906 to 1913. The garment that looks like a short-sleeved lacy cardigan was called a spencer and was a bodice that was worn underneath outer garments.

for women's combinations. All these innovations were the work of Pringle's famous frame-maker, Ben Wood.

On the knitwear side, argyle patterned socks were introduced and a cable stitch developed by Walter Pringle was used on a range of women's Norfolk coats, Pringle being one of the first firms to introduce knitted outerwear. In fact, in 1928 Pringle coined the term 'knitwear'.

Under the leadership of Robert Pringle (his father, Walter, had died in 1895), Pringle moved into the twentieth century. Almost its entire production was devoted to underwear, and in 1908 it developed a formula for unshrinkable underwear and guaranteed that all wool-and-silk and wool goods stamped with the trademark 'The "Rodono" Finish' that did shrink in washing would be replaced.

Meanwhile, experimentation in outerwear continued. The Edwardian age had brought a relaxation of manners and style. There was a craze among men and women for active sports such as cycling, tennis, golf and swimming, and there was a need for flexible informal clothing like the woman's knitted sports coat, a loose, long cardigan, often belted,

A 1910 men's underwear garment of the style that evolved into outerwear worn by sportsmen.

which came in about 1909 and was widely worn on informal occasions from then on.

Sportswear evolved from underwear that had absorbed sweat and prevented chills after exertion. People would actually turn their clothing inside out, as exemplified in the one-piece bathing suit, basically woollen combinations worn as outerwear. Other switches came when women began wearing their decorative lace-topped spencers (short-sleeved undergarments) on the outside as blouses and men began wearing their undershirts outside, which is when the 'sweater' was born.

By the end of the Edwardian era, Pringle brochures showed illustrations of gent's sweaters, women's knitted blouses and Norfolk jackets. There were also women's knitted coats with designs such as Teviot, Eildon, Glen and Mull.

The First World War caused Pringle to lose some momentum as it was occupied with producing sweaters, stockings and underwear for the Forces, but by 1917 industrially produced knitwear resembling the sweater as we know it today had become recognised as everyday apparel and was established as an important outerwear garment.

Apart from Robert Pringle & Son becoming a private limited company in 1922 (Walter Pringle's only son had died in the war), the 1920s were unremarkable for the company. The 1930s, however, were a different matter. They were exciting times for Pringle and the fashion trade. Courtiers Chanel, Patou and Lanvin gave knitwear the stamp of importance as sweater blouses and sweater suits became part of their collections twice a year. Schiaparelli launched her fashion career with sweaters and in America college girls adopted the 'sloppy joe' sweater, a long loose-knit garment. The sweater

A selection of women's Pringle knitwear in the early years of the twentieth century. Shown (right to left) is the Glen coat of 1910, a Norfolk jacket of 1910, a waistcoat of 1913 and a sports cardigan, also of 1913.

Gone are the old-fashioned golfing sweaters of the past – the Pringle of today is innovative and anything but conservative as this male kilt ensemble and show-string-strapped top with matching scarf show.

director of Marks & Spencer, as chief executive. When she took over the first thing to go was Faldo's £1.5 million a year sponsorship deal. As Kim realised that she had an amazing brand with a wonderful heritage and the potential to become great again, she employed visionaries rather than manufacturing experts who knew how to run a plant.

Pringle Scotland was relaunched as an international fashion brand in 2001 with its first flagship store opening in New Bond Street in London, making Pringle the oldest retailer in the street. A boutique was also opened in Terminal 3 at Heathrow Airport. Pringle then took on Japan with the opening of a retail store in the Ginza area of Tokyo. Expansion continued with the opening of London's Sloane Street store, which had an image of the new face of Pringle, curvaceous model Sophie Dahl, a modern version of a 1950s' sweater girl, sited on top of it.

Pringle also marked its new era as an international luxury brand with its first salon show at which garments such as bikinis, sexy off-the-shoulder cashmere sweaters and strapless twinsets were modelled.

Further shows saw sexy bandeau tops with matching hipster skirts, hot pants and bare-midriff cardigans. Although the mission was to revamp the brand's image, its Scottish heritage was retained, with the famous argyle pattern finding its way on to some of the garments. (The argyle pattern began with socks and was the result of an attempt to reproduce tartan in the looms.)

The new design direction came from one of Kim Winser's visionaries, Stuart Stockdale, appointed head designer in 2002. Aged 34, he was a graduate of the Central St Martins School of Design and the Royal College of Art, who had previously worked for the Italian designer Romeo Gigli, J. Crew of New York and Britain's Jasper Conran. Stockdale said it was an amazing opportunity to work for Pringle as it allowed him to combine his great interest in history with fashion. He found the extraordinary Pringle garment archive fascinating, and while his collections contained strong elements from the past, i.e. tradition and quality, they incorporated a high-fashion look to appeal to a younger, trendier market.

Celebrities create a market for

products, and an amazing bit of luck for Pringle came when David Beckham purchased four of their sweaters and wore one of them at a book-signing session. It could not have been better publicity and it cost nothing. Victoria Beckham was then seen wearing a Pringle jacket. More unsolicited publicity came when celebrities such as Pierce Brosnan, Madonna, Claudia Schiffer, Jamie Oliver and Robbie Williams were seen wearing Pringle garments.

In February 2000, Pringle was taken over by Hong Kong textile group SC Fang & Sons. When Pringle made a loss of £9 million in 2007, Fang embarked on a global restructuring, leading to the closure in 2008 of the plant in Hawick that had been in operation for almost 200 years. Production was transferred to Italy, where costs were 30 per cent lower than in Scotland. As the head office in Scotland was retained, the company was accused of only keeping it on so that it could continue to use the successful brand name Pringle of Scotland.

*Information and illustrations courtesy of Pringle.*

**ROBERTSON'S**

Robertson's is famous for the fine quality of its preserves and especially for its first product, 'Golden Shred' marmalade, whose origin goes back to 1864.

Born in 1832, the founder of the company, James Robertson, started his working life in a thread mill in Paisley. There was a recession in the industry, however, and as his future seemed insecure and he wished to become a shopkeeper, he left the mill, took a cut in salary and began an apprenticeship in 1847 with Messrs. Gibson and Craig, wine, spirit and tea merchants at 107–8 High Street. Being ambitious, during his apprenticeship he attended night-school classes at Seedhill School where he was taught reading, writing and arithmetic.

When he was twenty-seven, James Robertson achieved his ambition to have his own grocery shop. Little did he know, however, on that day in 1859 as he stood outside his premises at 86 Causeyside that he was destined to make the world's finest preserves.

Despite being shrewd in business, James was a kind, charitable man, and one day in 1864 he took pity on a struggling salesman and agreed to purchase a barrel of bitter oranges from him, even although he knew they would not sell well. He was right – sales of the oranges were very slow, and it would have ruined the tiny business if they could not be disposed of quickly. The solution came from his wife, Marion. Rather than see the oranges go to waste, she suggested that she should make them into marmalade to be sold in the shop.

Marion's tangy marmalade, clear with orange shreds throughout, was an immediate success and, realising the full business potential his enterprising wife had uncovered, James set about perfecting her recipe and somehow found a way to remove the bitterness of the orange while still retaining what he called 'the highly tonic value of the fruit'. This was the secret of the delicious Robertson's flavour and is the same secret that, even today, gives all Robertson's preserves their special flavour.

Marion Robertson is credited with coining the name 'Golden Shred', which James registered as his trademark for the clear type of marmalade for which the business became famous. She came up with the name as she held a jar of marmalade up to the window and was taken by the golden light filtering through the orange jelly and shreds of oranges. Later, a lemon marmalade named 'Silver Shred' was introduced, as well as jams and products such as 'Golden Shred' Mincemeat. Early advertisements for Robertson's Mincemeat pointed out that it should not be confused with butcher's minced beef as it was made from selected fruits, oriental spices and pure white sugar. Initially stone jars were used for the marmalade but were replaced by

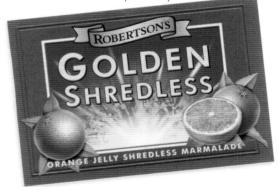

The current label for Golden Shredless marmalade.

1934 advertisement for Robertson's Mincemeat.

Street and built his first factory, which included a laboratory in which the produce was tested every half-hour.

With sales soon covering the whole of Britain and countries abroad, additional factories were opened: the famous jam works at Droylsden, near Manchester, in 1890; Catford, London, in 1900; and Brislington, Bristol, in 1914. There was also a plant in Boston, USA. So well thought of were Robertson's products that in 1907 Shackleton's Antarctic Expedition included Golden Shred in its supplies.

Until recently Robertson's trademark was their famous 'Golly', which first appeared in 1910 when one of James Robertson's sons, John, brought a Golly doll back from the USA and put its picture on the Robertson's price list. Soon afterwards the Golly symbol, with his red trousers, yellow waistcoat and blue, long-tailed jacket, was incorporated into every product label bearing the Robertson name.

The Golly badge scheme, which offered Golly enamel badges in a variety of different forms, starting with six different fruits, each with the Golly's head as part of the design, was run on each Robertson's label from 1928 to 2001. There was a short break during the Second

Right. 'A Breakfast Favourite the World Over'. A clever and colourful 1950s' advertisement for Golden Shred that shows the Robertson Golly seated at a table set on top of the world, which is shown as a giant orange with eyes, a nose and a mouth. When the Golden Shred drips from Golly's spoon, the orange's tongue sticks out to catch it. The slogan 'Robertson's Golden Shred Puts the Taste on the Toast' appeared on all advertisements.

glass jars in the 1930s.

When Marion's marmalade became so popular that the preserving pans in her kitchen were inadequate to cope with the demand, the couple decided to give up the grocery shop and start a

small factory. With typical Scottish ingenuity, they rented a section of a Paisley cloth-finishing works at Thrushgrove, where the surplus steam from the processing was used to heat the preserving pans. In 1880 James bought land in Stevenson

World War when the metal used to make the brooches was needed for the British war effort. Jolly Golly badges have featured famous golfers, cricketers, footballers, musicians and the Golly Lollipop Man, which appeared on all Robertson's road-safety materials produced for schoolchildren. The Golly badge scheme was the longest-running collector scheme in Britain. Over the years only minor changes, such as the positioning of the eyes and the smoothing of the hair, were made to the Robertson Golly, and although the logo has now gone it will not be forgotten.

Many fruits are used in the manufacture of Robertson's products – bitter or Seville oranges, lemons, redcurrants, blackcurrants, apricots, apples, plums, blackberries or 'brambles', raspberries, pineapples and damsons, which take their name from Damascus and have been cultivated in that area of the Middle East since before the Christian era. The use of 'bitter' or 'Seville' oranges in marmalade dates from the reign of Henry VII.

The Paisley factory closed in 1979, and in 1981 Robertson's was taken over by the Avana Food Group, which became part of RHM in 1987. Now part of Centura Foods, the company is one of the most successful producers of preserves in the world. The royal warrant, first presented to Robertson's by George V in 1933 and continued to the present time, is a testament to continued quality.

Above. Four famous Robertson labels – Golden Shred, Bramble Seedless, Silver Shred and Mincemeat. This advertisement dates from the 1960s at which time all these products were being manufactured in Paisley.

Left. 1950s' advertisement for Golden Shred with the emphasis on the product rather than the Robertson Golly trademark, as in the 'Orange' advertisement.

# ROSE'S LIME JUICE CORDIAL

Scotland gave the world its first concentrated bottled fruit drink – Rose's Lime Juice Cordial. It was the invention of Lachlan Rose, a member of a Leith family business of ship repairers and chandlery supplies. Lachlan, a younger son, had started up a second business in 1865 to provide food supplies to ships leaving Leith. It was called L. Rose and Company and specialised as lime and lemon juice merchants.

The reason behind the formation of the new company was that from 1795 it had been customary for ships of both the Merchant Marine and the Royal Navy to carry a supply of lime or lemon juice when on a long voyage to counteract the effects of scurvy. Scurvy is a deficiency disease caused by the absence of vitamin C, found in fresh fruit and vegetables. It was an Edinburgh doctor, James Lind, who discovered that a diet including citrus fruits was the most effective way of preventing scurvy, and when Captain Cook adopted the new treatment during his great expeditions of the 1770s, he lost only one man to scurvy in three years.

Because lime juice kept better than the juice of the other citrus juices that also contained vitamin C, the Merchant Shipping Act of 1867 made it compulsory for all British sailors on long sea voyages to be given a daily ration of lime juice to prevent scurvy, hence the sailors' nickname, 'Limeys'.

The year 1867 was also when Lachlan Rose patented the process for preserving lime juice without the addition of alcohol. Until then it was supplied to sailors laced with 15 per cent rum as a preserving agent. He had discovered that the preservative sulphur dioxide would prevent the juice from fermenting. He realised also that by adding sugar to his product and putting it in eye-catching bottles, he could market it to a wider public. Thus Rose's Lime Juice Cordial, the first branded fruit juice, was born.

L. Rose and Company went from strength to strength, 'furnishing delicious, cooling and refreshing beverages eminently suitable for family use'. As well as fruit juices, the range included exotic drinks with names like Ginger Brandy, Rum

Advertisement in *The Illustrated London News* of December 1934 for Rose's Lime Juice.

Shrub and Orange Quinine Wine.

The limes for Rose's Lime Juice were grown on the island of Dominica in the West Indies, and to ensure a regular supply in 1893 the company purchased its own estate on the island. It also developed plantations of lime trees in what is now Ghana in West Africa. Today the limes come from Peru or Mexico.

While the company started in Leith, in 1875 it transferred its headquarters to London and then in 1940 moved to St Albans to avoid the Blitz. When it moved to St Albans, it also opened a depot at Boxmoor, which is on the Grand Union Canal near Hemel Hempstead. Ships carrying concentrated lime juice would dock in the Port of London and, for convenience, the barrels of juice were loaded directly on to barges that travelled up the Thames and the Grand Union Canal to be unloaded at Boxmoor. As lime juice is no longer brought into the Port of London and the factory at St Albans has closed, barges are no longer required.

The secret of Rose's Lime Juice's unique flavour is a combination of the maturity of the fruit (seven years), the speed with which it is crushed – as soon as it falls off the trees – and the crushing process itself. After the limes are selected, they are washed in clear running water and then crushed between giant granite rollers in a mill.

Rose's has been part of the Schweppes portfolio since 1969, and although currently it is available only in lime in the UK, other flavours are available worldwide, where the brand is renowned as a premium cordial for use in cocktails.

Advertisement of 1947 for Rose's Lime Juice, which indicates that supplies were unavailable even two years after the end of the Second World War. Although their products were unavailable, to keep them alive in the public's mind companies continued to advertise them. This advertisement makes a point about the weather when the man says to the doctor, 'But I like my temperature. It's the first time I've been warm for months.' The year 1947 was one of the coldest on record, with freezing temperatures for months.

**ABSENTIA ROSEA**

"Bah! Do I really have to drink this, doctor?"

"Its function is to reduce the temperature to normal blood-heat."

"But I like my temperature. It's the first time I've been warm for months."

"You drink this now and you'll be fitter than a ferret in the morning."

"I say — you used just those words the night you intro-duced me to Rose's."

"Was it good advice?"

"The most Florence Nightingale act you ever did. By the way, when will Rose's Lime Juice be back again?"

"The most distressing condition known as 'absentia Rosea' is purely temporary. The symptoms suggest that complete recovery may be expected shortly."

**ROSE'S** — There is no substitute

# TENNENT'S LAGER

It is likely that anyone going for a pint in Glasgow will order a Tennent's lager, manufactured in the company's massive brewery in Duke Street, Glasgow. Tennent, as the city's oldest commercial business, is steeped in history, the Tennent family's connection with brewing going back to 1556 when Robert Tennent was a private brewer and maltser.

Until the beginning of the nineteenth century, ale, or 'yill' as it was known, was the staple drink of the Scots. Private maltmen brewed it

*Early Tennent beer labels.*

on a small scale and delivered it round the houses. Families of standing and innkeepers brewed their own. Robert Burns called it 'the puir man's wine'. Gradually, private brewing died out and public breweries appeared, one of these being H. & R. Tennent, founded in 1740 by brothers Hugh and Robert Tennent in rented premises in the Drygate area of Glasgow. Apart from it being a traditional area for brewing, as it was there that the monks had once brewed their ale, the reason the Drygate was so popular with brewers and maltsers was because of its close proximity

to the Molindinar Burn, which provided a vital ingredient – water. H. & R. Tennent's new brewery, however, had no need of the Molindinar, for it had its own supply of fresh clear water from a deep well within their property. It also had its own maltings and barley from the family farm of Easter Common (now the Petershill area of Glasgow).

H. & R. Tennent flourished, and it is recorded in city records that at Christmas 1745, on their way back from Derby, Prince Charles Edward Stuart and his bedraggled Jacobite army stopped at the brewery for sustenance. There they received ale

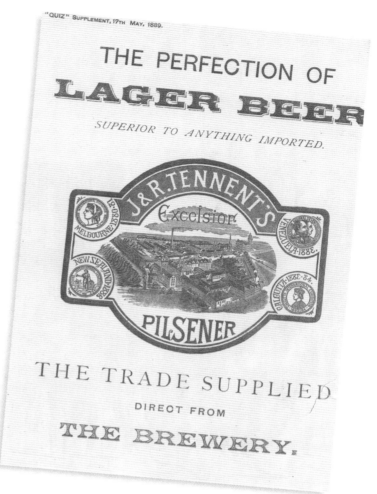

Advert of 1889 for J & R Tennent's pilsner lager beer stating that it was superior to anything imported. The new lager brewery had not been completed at the time.

and 'each and every man was refreshed and heartened by the brew'.

By the end of the eighteenth century the company's name had changed to J & R Tennent, the Drygate property had been bought, plus five acres of the adjacent Well Park lands, and an export trade had been established with large consignments of beer and stout going from the Clyde to North and South America.

The Victorian era was the most significant in the history of Tennent. By the 1850s, it had a large general business, a specialist trade in pale ales and stouts, and was the largest exporter of bottled beer in the world. In the 1860s, it began using what is probably Scotland's best-known brand symbol, the Tennent red 'T' trademark, registered in 1876 for sole use throughout the British Empire as the firm had large colonial sales as well as in the home market. In 1885, Hugh Tennent, aged twenty-

two, introduced the drink that revolutionised a nation's drinking habits – lager. Hugh suffered from tuberculosis and frequently convalesced in Europe. During a trip to Bavaria, he sampled the new light-coloured German beers that were threatening Tennent's Pale Ale market and decided that J & R Tennent should produce a similar product.

When Hugh returned home, his idea was laughed at. There was no way, everybody thought, that such a beer would be popular in Scotland. Nevertheless, Hugh was determined and in May 1885 the firm began brewing lager in a small way, using its existing plant. The

experiment was successful. Scotland took to the pale, sparkling light drink, and in 1889, Hugh commissioned a complete German lager brewery to be built alongside the existing ale brewery. To ensure its success, German brewer Jacob Klinger, who had been a consultant when lager brewing began, was put in charge of the venture, which a Glasgow newspaper condemned as 'a madman's dream'. Klinger chose engineering German contractor L.A. Reidinger of Ausburg, who had set up plants in places like Yokohama and Buenos Aires, to create Tennent's German-style brewery built entirely on a German model, even German coopers being

Advertisement for Tennent's Bombay Export Pale Ale.

imported to manufacture the cellar casks required for maturation.

The lager brewery was completed in 1891, but Hugh Tennent did not live to see his ambitious project become reality. He died in 1890, aged twenty-seven, and was the last member of the family to be in direct control of the company. His belief in a Scottish lager was justified, however, as in the 1890s, as well as the company winning many important awards, a German lager brewer described Tennent's lager as the best he had ever tasted.

The introduction of Tennent's lager ensured worldwide recognition for the Tennent brand, its reputation eventually rivalling that of its famous German, Danish and Dutch competitors.

Although throughout the years the lager has undergone many transformations, the brew drunk today is based on the original recipe. What has changed, though, is the way it is made. Today production is by up-to-date technology; then, it relied on manual labour with one group of workers giving rise to a derogatory Glaswegian expression. They were the women employed to clean the massive oak casks in which the lager was matured. Logically, they were known as 'scrubbers', a term that over the years became associated with women who could, at best, be described as a little rough.

When it comes to containers for its products, Tennent has always been in the forefront. By the end of the nineteenth century, it had its own pottery for the manufacture of the stoneware bottles then required for its products. It then went on to green or amber glass bottles, and in 1936 it was a pioneer of the 'beer can' when it introduced its cone-topped, crown-capped cans, affectionately known as 'Brasso' cans because of their similarity to a can of Brasso metal polish. Tennent's early beer cans were sold only to ships' stores.

The 'Brasso' cans were phased out after the Second World War, and in 1954 an American-style flat-topped can was introduced for the export market. A year later Tennent introduced the 'two-glass' sixteen-ounce can for the domestic market. 1959 to 1961 brought the Scottish Series (scenic views). 1962 brought the 'English Series' and 1964 saw the launch of the 'Housewives' Choice', twenty model girls, allegedly housewives, each accompanied by a recipe using beer.

Launched in January 1965, initially on the export market only, was the 'Ann Series', featuring Tennent's first can girl, model Ann Johansen, in various situations – at the pool, in the garden, sunbathing, boating on Loch Lomond. It was not the first time Ann had appeared on a Tennent can. She was the girl in the orange dress in the picture of Trafalgar Square from the 'English Series'. She was also one of the 'Housewives'. A second series, 'Ann's Day' – twelve scenes from a model's typical day – and a third, more risqué, series, 'Ann on Vacation', never appeared on the home market. The response to these series from men stationed overseas was phenomenal and thousands of

The 'Brasso' can, typical design of the time. Carried on the reverse was an assurance that the 'can opens like a bottle and pours like a bottle', and that it 'cools quickly and takes up less space in the refrigerator or ice box'.

The first Lager Lovelies:
very demure!

Left. A show card of the late 1950s showing a delectable young lady and the two-glass can, which has hardly changed since its introduction in 1955.

Right. One of the cans from the series 'Ann on Vacation', confined to the export market as the pictures were considered too risqué for the home market.

letters were received requesting prints. From 1965 to 1969 Ann featured on every can of lager and export sold by Tennents, and on every can of lager and stout until 1974 and 1980 respectively.

In 1969, the best-known advertising campaign in the history of canned beer, Tennent's famous 'Lager Lovelies', replaced Ann on the lager cans. For the export market, they were called Tennent's Girls. The original Lovelies were Linda, Pat, Angela, Susan and Vicky. Among subsequent Lovelies were beauty queens Marie Kirkwood and Lorraine Davidson, both of whom had held the Miss Scotland title. In 1982, all the current Lovelies appeared in the 300 poses that made up the 'Can Girl Calendar', obtained by sending in twelve

special ring-pulls. The offer was open for less than three months during which 30,000 calendars were requested. To celebrate their lager centenary in 1985, Tennent produced a series of special cans showing Lager Lovelies as they might have looked at various times in history.

Prominent though they were, the Lager Lovelies were just part of an integrated advertising campaign for Tennent's products, involving billboards, press and award-winning TV advertising such as the brash, exuberant, catchy 'Tennent's Special' commercials.

Although no more, the Lager Lovelies are not forgotten as their cans are in the hands of collectors worldwide and are avidly sought after.

Almost as famous as the lager girls is Tennent's red T trademark, which can be seen everywhere from rock festivals to advertising hoardings. The company sponsors T in the Park, Scotland's biggest music festival, the first taking place in 1993. The company also sponsors the Tennent's Scottish Cup football tournament.

At the beginning of 2003, Tennent Caledonian Breweries was voted Glasgow's favourite business, a great boost for the brand and the people who work in the establishment. Tennent is owned by the Belgian brewing giant Interbrew, the second largest brewer in the world.

*Information and illustrations courtesy of Tennent*

While The Royal Bank of Scotland received its royal charter of Incorporation on 31 May 1727, its beginnings lie in the Act of Union in 1707 when England agreed to pay Scotland a pecuniary 'Equivalent' of £398,085 10s. sterling in compensation for the disastrous Darien expedition and other losses and bets arising from the Union. In addition, Scotland was to receive a proportion of the increase in tax revenue expected to result from the Union – the 'Arising Equivalent' as it was called. When the Equivalent arrived in Edinburgh, however, only £100,000 instead of the expected £400,000 was in coin, and it was only after protest that another £50,000 was sent from London. As £150,000 was insufficient to compensate all the creditors in coin, many had to be satisfied with debentures – the government's

promise to pay at some future date with interest.

Two societies of debenture holders were formed, one in London and one in Edinburgh, but both were wound up in 1724 when the Equivalent Company, registered in Scotland, was created. Soon the directors of the new company wished to extend its rudimentary banking services beyond the membership of the defunct societies. They wanted to look after other people's money as well as their own. They wanted the company to become a bank. Consequently, the Equivalent Company applied for a charter in banking in Scotland only. South of the border the Bank of England held an unbreakable monopoly, but in Scotland the Bank of Scotland's twenty-one years of monopoly had expired in 1716 and had not been

renewed. The name 'Equivalent' was dropped, and a charter incorporating The Royal Bank of Scotland was granted on 31 May 1727 under the great seal of Scotland.

The Royal Bank of Scotland opened for business on 8 December 1727 at the foot of Ship Close in Edinburgh (now Old Stamp Office Close). It had a capital of £111,347 and authority to 'exercise the rights and powers of banking' in Scotland. As extra capital, the new bank called up £22,000 from its subscribers as a banking fund. It also gained control of £20,000, representing the belated payment under the Act of Union whereby the government was required to pay that amount to Scotland to be lent out at interest for the improvement of fisheries and general manufacturing. Opportunely, the whole sum was deposited with The Royal Bank

An early Royal Bank ledger that includes the entry for the first cash credit, granted to William Hogg Junior. Resting on the ledger are pocket scales used to check the weight of coins that might have been filed or clipped. Also shown are notes and coins of the time, including The Royal Banks' guinea note and an 'option clause' note.

companies, thereby pioneering correspondent banking in Scotland. Without branches, however, the expansion of its note issue proved difficult, and a new approach was adopted. The bank's links with Glasgow, where it had been closely involved in financing the tobacco trade, had been strong from the outset, and in 1783 it opened a branch in a small shop at Hopkirk's Land near Glasgow Cross. The timing was right, for the Glasgow banks had lost much of their drive and invested much of their funds in government loans.

Robert Scott Moncrieff and David Dale, appointed joint Glasgow agents, established a huge business in the discount of bills of exchange, thereby altering the entire balance of the bank's affairs and accounting for at least half its business. Indeed, within a few years The Royal Bank dominated the Glasgow banking scene. Glasgow remained the bank's only branch office for fifty years, and during that time, being involved in servicing the profitable cotton and

as the chairman and the majority of the trustees and commissioners of the board had been Equivalent proprietors. The old bank, the Bank of Scotland, had expected to receive half of it on interest.

The new bank had a staff of eight – the Cashier, the Secretary and his Clerk, the Accountant and his Clerk, two Tellers and a Messenger. The first Governor was the Earl of Ilay (later Duke of Argyll), one of the most powerful men in Scotland and instrumental in securing the charter.

Immediately the new bank embarked on a ruthless and vigorous campaign to destroy the Bank of Scotland (established in 1695) by the collection and presentation of large quantities of its notes, and by May 1728 the two banks were frostily negotiating a possible merger. Unable to agree to merge, however, the two banks resigned themselves to an uneasy coexistence.

In 1728 The Royal Bank invented the 'cash credit', forerunner of the overdraft, whereby a merchant of good standing, backed

by his own bond and that of responsible friends, could borrow more than he had deposited. Soon afterwards the bank also began to accept deposits at interest, although note issue remained the focus of its lending and profits for several decades.

Instead of establishing branches, The Royal Bank developed connections with the growing number of provincial banking

Print showing the Stirling Mansion (originally the Cunninghame Mansion) when it belonged to The Royal Bank of Scotland. The mansion, with a portico added to the front and an extension to the rear, is now the home of GOMA, the Gallery of Modern Art. The building to the right in the illustration is the Theatre Royal, which burned down in 1829.

Engraving of c.1820s of The Royal Bank's registered office, Dundas House in St Andrew Square, Edinburgh. The house was build in 1772 for Sir Lawrence Dundas of Kerse, then Governor of The Royal Bank. Sir Lawrence died in 1781, and thirteen years later the house was sold to the government and became the principal office of Excise in Scotland. In 1825 the Crown sold the house to The Royal Bank of Scotland which, in the 1850s, added the magnificent rear domed banking hall. The coat of arms in the pediment dates from when the house was the excise office and is the royal coat of arms of George III. It remains on the building because of a ruling by the Lord Lyon that it is a right belonging to the property rather than to the institution that occupies it.

quartered there for more than a week with triple sentries at the gates. As the bank held much of the city's valuable plate and treasure, it was regarded as 'The Mint' or 'The Tower' of Glasgow.

In 1819 the bank's headquarters moved from Edinburgh's congested Old town to St Andrew Square in the New Town, occupying from 1825 a magnificent townhouse built in 1772 for Sir Lawrence Dundas of Kerse, then Governor of The Royal Bank. This building is still the bank's registered office.

During the early years of the nineteenth century it became clear that the restriction of the bank's note issue to Edinburgh and Glasgow would curtail the future growth of the business, and by 1836 six branches had been opened in Dundee, Rothesay, Dalkeith, Greenock, Port Glasgow and Leith. After the collapse of the Western Bank in 1857 The Royal acquired a number of its agencies and in 1864 the Dundee Banking Co. was acquired.

In 1874, authorised by a private Act of Parliament, The Royal Bank followed the example of other Scottish banks by opening a branch in London. Four years later, the disastrous collapse of the City of Glasgow Bank left the Scottish banking world shaken. The manager, secretary and six directors of the City of Glasgow Bank were arrested on a charge of fraud, tried and jailed.

sugar trades, it produced more business than any other bank office in the UK outside London.

The Glasgow branch of The Royal moved into the Stirling Mansion in Queen Street and when, during the radical uproar of 1820, there were fears that the mob would plunder the bank, Captain Smith's Guard of Sharpshooters was

Poster c.1930s advertising The Royal Bank's foreign exchange services.

Introduced by the National Bank of Scotland, Britain's first mobile bank gets its first customer, a representative from the Harris Tweed Association.

A positive result of the disaster, however, was the adoption by all the banks of the practice of having their accounts and balance sheets audited by professional independent accountants. Despite difficult trading conditions, during the last years of the nineteenth century The Royal Bank continued to thrive, and by 1910 it had 158 branches and around 900 employees.

The declaration of war with Germany on 4 August 1914 brought uncertainty to banking. A royal proclamation extended the bank holiday period for three days, and a moratorium was declared under which the obligation of the banks to pay their depositors was temporarily suspended. The banks were drawn into funding the government's war loans and advances, and note issue increased rapidly. As small denomination notes were in great demand, special Treasury notes of £1 and ten shillings were issued. (Five pounds had been the smallest Bank of England note.) Scottish bank notes, where £1 notes were the norm, were declared legal tender both north and south of the border for the duration of hostilities. Many bank officers and clerks of military age enlisted, and temporary junior clerks and the recruitment of female staff on an unprecedented scale filled the gaps. Overall, the volume of banking business grew during the war, prompting a series of major amalgamations in 1918, including moves to affiliate some Scottish and English banks.

After the war, The Royal embarked upon a policy of expansion in London, acquiring Drummonds Bank in 1924, Williams Deacon's Bank in 1930 and the old London Bank of Glyn, Mills & Co. in 1939 when war was imminent.

During the Second World War the bank experienced similar problems as in the previous war, with controls over foreign exchange and lending priorities and the marketing and distribution of savings certificates and defence bonds.

Expansion continued during the 1950s and 60s, with the opening of new branches in Scotland and London and the launch of new services such as personal loans and cash dispensers. By 1968 economic pressures led to further consolidation, and in 1969 The Royal Bank of Scotland merged with the National Commercial Bank of Scotland. After the merger, the new Royal Bank, with 693 branches, enjoyed over 40 per cent of Scotland's banking business. The National Commercial had been a fusion of the National Bank of Scotland Ltd (established 1825) and the Commercial Bank of Scotland Ltd (established 1810) in 1959. The National Bank of Scotland had pioneered mobile banking services with the introduction in 1946 of a

biscuits, which were then transferred to the chocolate-enrobing machine, cooled and then wrapped by hand in aluminium foil. The girls made 2,500 three-dozen boxes of Tea Cakes per week.

While Archie Tunnock created all the new products, their success was a joint effort between father and sons. It was Archie, however, who realised the importance of having the right packaging. While at first he sent out wafers and mallows in plain cardboard boxes, he discovered that for one penny more he could have gaily coloured containers with cut-out lids that folded into attractive display stands. 'That bit of colour,' he said, 'almost doubled my sales overnight.'

Advertising has played a big part in Tunnock's success. Sales of their products have risen and fallen in relation to the amount of advertising undertaken. In the 1950s Archie offered a Ford saloon car plus £1,000 in prizes to inventors of names for biscuits. Even the company's fleet of red and black painted vans, bearing the driver's name on the back, are a well-known trademark.

Archie Tunnock continued to take a close interest in the business until his death in 1981 at the age of eighty-six. By then both his sons, Tom and Boyd, were running the company. Tom died in 1992, and Boyd is in charge of the company, helped by his daughters, Karen and Fiona, the fourth generation of Tunnocks to be involved with the company.

Tunnock turn out four million Caramel Wafers every week, three million Tea Cakes, one million Snowballs and one million Caramel Logs. Each day fifteen tons of

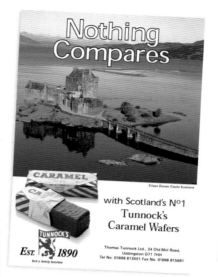

Advertisement of 1999 for Caramel Wafers featuring Eilean Donan Castle, Scotland. This advertisement was one of a series headed 'Nothing Compares'.

caramel is produced and, together with full cream milk and chocolate, it makes the company's best-selling line, Caramel Wafers. The wafers are a worldwide household name, and each week well over three million are exported to more than thirty countries, including Saudi Arabia, Japan, the United States, Canada, Hong Kong, Trinidad and the West Indies. Newfoundland was the first export market. One of the firm's secrets is that, however hot the climate, none of the chocolate sticks to the wrapper. Boyd Tunnock received an MBE in recognition of export achievements. 'It stands for My Biscuits are Enjoyable,' he joked. While he would be the first to say that his company's products are the best, Boyd has been known to confess that he loves KitKats. Like his father and grandfather, he puts in long hours and for relaxation sails his yacht *Lemarac* ('Caramel' backwards). Enough said.

As well as its famous products, the factory, which employs around

Advertisement for Milk Chocolate Tea Cakes that appeared in trade magazines and as posters in London where it sent up the Millennium Dome.

600 townspeople, produces a full range of traditional Scottish products for the Tunnock tearoom in Uddingston. For decades Tunnock has been famous for its wedding cakes, and there is a special section for making these and other celebration cakes. A full-time artist decorates them, an intricate part of the work being the hand-modelling of tiny figures in sugar.

Every year offers to buy the company arrive, and the Tunnock family could stop working immediately. All approaches are rejected, which speaks volumes.

*Information and illustrations courtesy of Tunnocks.*

The arrival of the Ultimo bra took the lingerie market by storm. At last, women were able to get the cleavage enhancement they wanted without the discomfort normally associated with cleavage-enhancing products. Ultimo, the ultimate bra, achieves the 'cleavage with ultimate comfort' thanks to the silicone gel cushions, containing a secret ingredient, that are sewn into the bra. When worn the gel adapts to the contours of the body to form comfortable pads underneath the breasts, pushing them together and upwards. Because of the gel, the bra offers a look and feel that is natural and allows movement.

Ultimo was the brainchild of Glasgow girl Michelle Mone who, because of an illness in the family, left school aged fifteen with no qualifications. Too young for full-time employment, at 5 feet 10 inches tall she got a job as a fashion model.

At the age of twenty, Michelle got married and, after giving birth to her first child, she decided that she wanted to gain business experience. She took a job with Labatt's Beer Company, starting as an office junior. Two years later she was running its Scottish sales and marketing team. Two years on, however, Labatt closed down its UK operation, making Michelle redundant.

In October 1996 Michelle went to a dinner dance with her husband, wearing a very uncomfortable cleavage-enhancing bra. This was when she decided she could invent a bra that could offer women the cleavage enhancement they wished but be so comfortable that they could wear it every day. (Later, in an interview, she said that if she had had a perfect bust, the Ultimo bra would never have been invented.) Having convinced her husband that this was a viable business idea and worth investing her redundancy money in, she set up MJM International Ltd in November 1996.

Prominence came quickly for MJM when, a year after it was launched, it won the title of Business Start-Up of the Year, awarded by the Glasgow Development Agency. In 1998, because of Michelle's marketing skills, contacts and force of personality, MJM beat off competition from other leading companies and won the contract to market, sell and distribute ELLE's range of underwear and nightwear in the UK.

Meanwhile, Michelle was working on the product for which she was to become famous – Ultimo, the ultimate bra. It took her nearly three years to invent it, working with a team of European bra technicians. Finally, in August 1999, MJM International launched the gel-filled Ultimo bra in Selfridges, London, to great acclaim. It was the biggest bra launch ever in the UK. There were over fifty photographers and camera crews from the UK, Europe and even CNN for the USA. Selfridges sold out six weeks' stock of Ultimo within twenty-four hours.

When Ultimo was launched in May 2000 in the exclusive Saks Fifth Avenue store in New York, there was a six weeks' waiting list for it.

The press coverage received by both Michelle and Ultimo was incredible. She has a huge cupboard in her office packed with newspaper and magazine articles and videos of TV appearances. Her dream when she started MJM was to appear with Ultimo in her local evening paper, the Glasgow *Evening Times*. When

Rachael Hunter wearing the innovative Miracle Body undergarment which gives women a cleavage when wearing backless and virtually frontless dresses.

Supermodel Rachael Hunter wearing the famous Ultimo plunge bra and matching briefs.

she appeared in America's top weekly magazine, *People*, which sells over fifty million copies, her expectations were surpassed. She was further delighted to discover that actress Julia Roberts wore Ultimo to enhance her cleavage in the film *Erin Brockovich*.

As well as phenomenal press coverage, accolades came fast and furious for Michelle, especially in 2000. In April, at the Epcot Centre, Florida, she won the coveted World Young Business Achiever award, beating off top entrepreneurs from fourteen countries. In October she became Business Woman of the Year at the Corporate Elite Awards, and in November she won the *Sunday Mail* Great Scot of the Year Business Award. In 2001 she won the Best Newcomer category at the British Apparel Export Awards. In addition, in 2001, Prince Charles asked Michelle to join his board of directors for the Prince's Trust Scotland.

The Ultimo collection, which as well as the Ultimo bra, includes underwear, swimwear and nightwear, has won over twenty-one competitions and has beaten Wonderbra every time. The range is available worldwide, including Japan, the USA, Sweden, Norway, France, Malta, Iceland and Singapore. An innovative addition to the range was introduced in 2003. It was the Miracle Body, a hi-tech garment that gives women a cleavage when wearing backless and virtually frontless dresses.

Michelle Mone is recognised as being among the top thirty women entrepreneurs in the UK. Not bad for a girl who left school aged fifteen and with no qualifications.

*Information and illustrations courtesy of MJM International.*

# WALKERS SHORTBREAD

While some Scottish companies play down their Scottishness when trying to capture international markets, not so Walkers of Aberlour, which exports 45 per cent of its products. It is the only UK biscuit company to reach that figure. Sold in more than 65 widely spread overseas markets, Walkers shortbread is recognised as being the finest in the world and the company proudly proclaims its origins by giving its products a distinctive red tartan packaging and a logo showing a picture of Bonnie Prince Charlie and Flora Macdonald. It believes that traditional products should have traditional packaging. While the packaging is certainly eye-catching, however, the company's success is down to the continued excellence of its products, produced at three factories in Aberlour and one in Elgin.

Walkers, the largest family-run UK biscuit manufacturer, was established in 1898 by Joseph Walker who, with the help of a £50 loan, opened a village bakery in Torphins, near Banchory in Aberdeenshire. He was only twenty-one and had served an apprenticeship with Mitchell & Muil's bakery in Aberdeen. Joseph had very high standards, and as he had his mind set on creating the world's finest shortbread, he spent his first year in business perfecting his recipe.

Thanks to the excellence of his products, Joseph's bakery thrived, and in addition to his local year-round customers, those who visited the district during the fishing and

This photograph was taken in 1898, the year Joseph Walker started his business in Torphins at the age of twenty-one.

Joseph Walker, left, outside his shop in Torphins around 1908, with two horse vans.

shooting seasons would find their way to his shop. The lodges and grand houses, famous for their lavish entertaining when occupied by shooting parties, were also valuable sources of local trade. The Edwardian era was the heyday of the sporting estate, and the Speyside area was favoured because of its climate, setting and good rail connections. Even King Edward VII shot there regularly.

Demand for Joseph's products grew so rapidly that in 1909 he moved to a larger shop in Aberlour, which still trades today, selling bread, rolls and other bakery goods.

As the years went by Joseph's business prospered, and after the First World War his two sons, Joseph and James, joined him in the shop. James had trained in Kennaway's of Aberdeen, which had a high reputation for the confectionery side of the bakery trade.

In the countryside, the motor van played an important part in meeting customers' needs and Walkers' first was a Model T Ford purchased in 1923. Orders were also sent as far afield as Dalwhinnie by way of the old Speyside railway line.

By the mid-1930s, not only was the day-to-day trade such as bread and biscuits doing well, but there was a remarkable demand for shortbread and cakes. Clearly, Walkers insistence on using only the finest flour, butter and other natural commodities in its products had paid off. By the start of the Second World War, shortbread was packaged in tins, making it even more transportable. Unlike the colourful tins of today, however, the first ones were plain with a printed-

An advertisement of 1973 for Walkers Highlander Shortbread which was a more rugged type of shortbread – thicker, more crunchy and rolled in demerara sugar.

*A Highlander and proud of it*

Walkers' shortbread gift tins in their distinctive red tartan bearing classic romantic paintings from Scotland's historic past capture the traditions of chivalry and rebellion that shaped a nation.

paper wrapper.

The post-war years saw gradual expansion, and to correct the high labour cost of producing the general baking lines, it was decided in the mid-1950s to concentrate on the production of shortbread, it being less labour-intensive in proportion to the ingredient cost.

Expansion continued, and by the 1960s James Walker's three children, Joseph, James and Marjorie, had entered the company and were taking responsibility for running and developing it. By the end of the 1960s the business was supplying most of Speyside via its twenty vans and shops in Grantown-on-Spey, Elgin, Aviemore and Aberlour.

As the demand for shortbread had increased dramatically, to take advantage of markets throughout the UK the pure-butter shortbread was given an increased shelf-life by improved watertight packaging that kept the product in perfect condition, preserving the fresh bakery taste for a year. By then the company was supplying such important shops as Harrod's and Fortnum and Mason.

Despite the 1970s being economically difficult for Scotland, Walkers continued to expand, with a move to a purpose-built factory at the edge of Aberlour village in 1975. The company had moved into the export market by then, and it had become obvious that the business could not continue operating from its original premises even although these had had a 25,000-square-foot extension tacked on.

Overseas sales became so successful that Walkers received the Queen's Award for Export Achievement three times. It is the highest award given to British exporters, and Walkers is the only British food company to gain such a distinction. In 1987 Walkers received the first ever Highland Business Award, granted to the company making the greatest contribution to the economy of the Highlands of Scotland. Recognition also came from Europe with Monde Selection in Geneva awarding Gold Medals for Walkers' products in 1986 and 1989. In January 2002 Walkers received its first royal warrant for the supply of oatcakes to the Queen.

Walkers' packaging has come a long way from plain tins with printed-paper wrappers, for today, as well as carrying a distinctive red tartan, it features, among others, a famous painting of Flora MacDonald saying farewell to Bonnie Prince Charlie, the most romantic moment of Scottish history. Since the 1960s this image has stared out at us from every outlet where Walkers' products are on sale. The Walker family had seen it in a book, liked it and, as it was out of copyright, decided to use it. Although the company was using the painting, however, it did not own it and had no idea who did until, at the beginning of 1998, it received a phone call from Sotheby's in London to say that 'their' painting was up for auction and would Walkers be interested in bidding. Fortunately,

Walkers were successful in purchasing the painting, and it now proudly hangs in the company's boardroom.

Apparently, the reason for the name 'shortbread' is that before sugar was produced people baked bread made from a tough elastic dough. After sugar became available in the seventeenth century, they were also able to make a type of biscuit that was called 'shortbread' because it was short (crumbly in texture) and easily broken. Some say that the patterned edge on a shortbread round symbolises the sun's rays and originates from the early days of sun worship. Later, Yule-bread, a thin bannock (circle) of oatmeal with a notched edge, was baked during Christmas and Hogmanay.

Shortbread has also had a French input. When Mary Queen of Scots returned to Scotland to ascend the throne she brought her French chef with her. He took the thick round shapes of traditional shortbread and altered them to make them more delicate, giving us what we know today as Petticoat Tails, the name coming from the French *petites gatelles*.

Walkers produces over thirty varieties of shortbread. As well as the traditional fingers, there are specialised flavoured shortbreads such as ginger, vanilla, hazelnut, almond and chocolate-coated. There are even mini-shortbreads bursting with dark and white chocolate chips. An organic range was introduced, baked to the original recipe but using only organic flour, butter and sugar.

As well as shortbread, the company's products include traditional biscuits, oatcakes and

The cake that's a 'dram' come true. Walkers' rich fruit cake, which has Glenfiddich single malt whisky added to the mix.

meringues. There are also cakes, like a deliciously rich and moist fruit cake that has Glenfiddich single malt whisky added to the mix. The Glenfiddich cake is produced in association with the famous distillery lying near Walkers in the Spey Valley.

Walkers is an outstanding example of what Scotland has to offer. Its story is one of admirable success brought about by never compromising on quality and by marketing its products superbly. Joseph Walker succeeded in making the world's best shortbread, a tradition being carried on today by his descendants who own and manage the company.

*Illustrations courtesy of Walkers.*

# WHITE HORSE WHISKY

The history of White Horse is linked with the island of Islay, off the west coast of Scotland, during the old days of smuggling. There the enterprising Johnstone family operated ten separate 'bothies', little one-room huts in which illicit stills produced *uisge beatha*, the Gaelic for 'the water of life' – whisky. Islay was one of the principal sources of illicit liquor, an illegal trade that flourished until 1816 when John Johnstone combined the ten bothies into a legal distillery called Lagavulin, taken from Gaelic and meaning 'the mills in the hollow'.

The Graham family succeeded the Johnstone family at Lagavulin and joined forces with James Logan Mackie to create the firm of J. L. Mackie & Co. Mackie, a relative of the Grahams, had started his business career in the 1840s with Alexander Graham, a Glasgow spirit merchant and agent for Lagavulin and Laphroaig Distillers in Islay, which were owned by his brother, Walter. When Alexander Graham retired in 1850, Mackie took over the business, trading under his own name. It was some time later that Mackie joined forces with the

Graham family at Lagavulin.

In 1878 a man who became one of the great pioneers and personalities of the Scotch whisky industry joined J. L. Mackie & Co. He was James Mackie's nephew, Peter Jeffrey Mackie, who was sent to learn his craft at Lagavulin where he developed a passionate and lifelong interest in whisky distilling.

Following his training, Peter

The eccentric Peter Jeffrey Mackie.

Mackie developed his uncle's business into one of the world's great whisky firms. He became the senior partner in 1890 and, determined that the firm should start blending, and set up a new company, Mackie & Co., for that purpose. The blends, made up in bulk in the company's warehouses, were sold to breweries and spirit merchants in the south of England. Later, J. L. Mackie & Co. and Mackie & Co. were amalgamated to form Mackie & Co (Distillers).

Peter Mackie was the first to recognise the importance of maintaining a continuous standard of whisky and a brand name for it, and in 1890 he registered his own brand, 'Mackie's White Horse Cellar Scotch Whisky'.

An amalgam of Highland history and atmosphere inspired Mackie to choose the name White Horse for his product, the name and the date on the label, 1742, deriving from one of the most famous ancient inns – the White Horse Cellar in the Canongate of Edinburgh, close to the Mackie family home. (Although it had property in the Canongate, the White Horse

The White Horse Inn in Edinburgh's Canongate – 1745.

Cellar never belonged to the Mackie family, as once claimed in the company's advertising.) Patronised by literary and theatrical notables, the inn served as a favourite off-duty rendezvous for officers of Prince Charles Edward Stuart's Highland Army when it was quartered in Edinburgh during the rebellion of 1745, and was steeped in history. It was from here that the stagecoach to London would set off at five in the morning every Monday and Friday, a journey proudly advertised in February 1745 as taking eight days (God permitting) and granting intrepid travellers the privilege of a fourteen pound luggage allowance.

There is more than one explanation as to how the inn got its name. One is that White Horse Close, which housed the inn, was named after the white palfrey that carried Mary Queen of Scots to and from the nearby Palace of Holyroodhouse. Another is that it was named for a white horse owned by the innkeeper, which won a race on Leith sands, saving its owner from bankruptcy. In gratitude, the innkeeper was said to have kept the horse idle for the rest of its days besides setting up its portrait in his sign.

Peter Mackie's White Horse

Whisky was initially sold only in export markets and was not launched on the home market until 1902 where, within five years, it sold 27,000 cases. Sales continued to

This American advertisement for White Horse appeared in *New Yorker* magazine in October 1938.

climb, and by the outbreak of the First World War it was the favourite whisky of countless army messes and had a strong position in both the home and export markets.

As well as producing his own brand of whisky, over the years Peter Mackie acquired distilleries – Lagavulin which the company inherited in 1889; Craigellachie in 1915, which Mackie and a partner built in 1892; and Hazelburn in 1920. At Hazelburn, Mackie set up a laboratory where Masataka Taketsuru learned the craft of whisky distilling that enabled him to set up Suntory and Nikka in Japan. Mackie would hold his annual

289492

YOUR INDEX TO QUALITY

For your protection every bottle of White Horse Scotch bears an individual number, which indicates exactly when the Scotch in that bottle was made, blended, bottled and shipped. This ensures a check on perfect uniformity! Never too heavy • Never too light • White Horse always tastes just right!

WHITE HORSE

BLENDED SCOTCH WHISKY 86.8 PROOF • A BLEND OF 100% SCOTCH WHISKIES ALL 8 YEARS OLD • BROWNE VINTNERS CO., INC., N.Y.

"*I can tell it blindfold...*

## It's equal to a fine liqueur"

The outstanding qualities of White Horse are everywhere recognised and approved. The tempting aroma, the rare peat and heather flavour and the softness given by age are the unmistakable signs of the whisky that is acclaimed to be equal to a fine liqueur.

*Millions and millions of gallons maturing*

# WHITE HORSE
# WHISKY

*Half bottles and small flasks on sale.*

One of the successful 'I can tell it blindfold' advertisements of the 1930s.

general meetings at Craigellachie, during which he would forcefully air his opinions on the industry and the British Empire. Another Mackie venture, rather odd, was the production of BBM flour, ground from 'bran, bone and mussel', which all members of staff were required to use in their homes.

Known as 'Restless Peter', Peter Mackie was described as 'one third genius, one third megalomaniac, and one third eccentric'. His philosophy was clear: 'As in other things, there are good and bad whiskies. If we cannot afford to buy the best, especially in the matter of Scotch whisky, we should save our money and go without.' He met all cautionary advice with the words 'Nothing is impossible', a term that became a byword within the company. He was a champion of high standards in Scotch whisky and a great fighter for the cause of allowing whiskies to mature. He was a passionate Conservative and an outspoken critic of Lloyd George, then Chancellor of the Exchequer, whom he referred to as 'a Welsh country solicitor' for his attacks on the whisky trade and for the imposition of punishing taxes on Scotch whisky. Lloyd George was teetotal, and during the First World War declared drink to be a deadlier enemy than Germany and Austria. Mackie also ridiculed the Cabinet during the war, accusing them of 'frittering their time in war films and having themselves in cinema shows'. Despite this, Mackie accepted a baronetcy in 1920 from Lloyd George's coalition government.

After Peter Mackie's only son was killed during the First World War, he threw himself into the promotion of White Horse Whisky. He regarded the whole world as his marketplace and travelled it in search of new outlets for the brand, setting up White Horse as a market leader in many countries. It was even available in the United States during Prohibition. Whisky was legally imported into the country as medicine and American doctors prescribed White Horse for medicinal purposes. This was not the first time whisky had been advocated for medicinal purposes. During the influenza epidemic following the First World War, green and gold stamps were issued by

White Horse bearing the words: Alcohol The Only Remedy for Influenza – Scotch Whisky for Preference. Such advertising is prohibited today as it is socially irresponsible to link alcohol with medicinal properties.

Under Mackie's leadership White Horse achieved an international status that never diminished, establishing great prestige both for the brand and the Scotch whisky industry as a whole. Restless and eccentric he may have been, but a notice in his Glasgow office summed Mackie up – one side said 'Honesty is the best policy', the other said 'Take nothing for granted'.

When Peter Mackie died in 1924 the name of the company was changed to White Horse Distillers, making White Horse Whisky a rare example of a product that later gave its name to its producer. In 1926 the company pioneered screw caps, which took the marketplace by storm and doubled the sales of the brand in six months. Before then bottles had been corked. Three years after Mackie's death, the Distillers Company Ltd, which he had always prevented buying his business, bought it, completing the amalgamation of the Big Five – James Buchanan & Co., John Dewar & Sons, Haig & Co., John Walker & Sons and White Horse Distillers.

While Peter Mackie was not keen on advertising, believing the quality of the whisky was the most important factor in selling it, the brand, now owned by Diageo, went on to have innovative advertising campaigns like the popular 'I can tell it blindfold' series of advertisements. These featured gentlemen 'nosing the whisky' with bandages over their eyes. A later series of clever and

One of the popular 'You can take a White Horse anywhere' advertisements of the 1960s and 1970s.

witty advertisements were those of the 'You can take a White Horse anywhere' campaign.

The top-rated White Horse, whose key malts in the blend are Glen Elgin and Lagavulin, enjoys an international reputation. It has won many awards for excellence and is shipped to various countries where Scotch whisky drinkers appreciate its distinctive taste. Peter Mackie's legacy lives on in his White Horse Whisky.

*Information and illustrations courtesy of Diageo.*

# WILLIAM YOUNGER'S BEER

William Younger & Co. owed its beginnings to sixteen-year-old William Younger, who left his home in Linton, Peeblesshire, in 1749 to work as a brewer in Leith.

There are conflicting details of William's start as a brewer. *The Younger Centuries* by David Keir, a

William Younger, the founder of what became Scottish & Newcastle plc.

book on the first 200 years of William Younger & Co., says that he started up a small kitchen brewery somewhere near the Kirkgate. A more recent book, *Good Company* by Berry Ritchie, the story of Scottish & Newcastle, states that he went to work in Robert Anderson's brewery near St Anthony's Church, Leith. Regardless of where William did begin his brewing in 1753 he gave it up to become an exciseman.

Apart from his pay as an exciseman, William received a percentage of the money realised on the goods he seized, and as his earnings increased, he invested in land, property, a share in a ship, a partnership in a stagecoach company and a brewery. By 1769, however, William was overworked and ill, and on 5 May 1770 he died, aged thirty-seven.

William left his widow, Grizel, £4,270 Scots (worth about £350 sterling then) plus his property and business investments, and while this made her well off, she had five children – three boys and two girls – to support. Of all her husband's business interests, Grizel thought the brewery seemed most likely to

provide a living for her family, so she sold his other enterprises, advertised herself as Mrs Grizel Younger the brewer and took her eldest son, Archibald, on as an apprentice.

The Younger story now moves to William's three sons, Archibald, Richard and William, who all set up brewing businesses. Archibald was the first to do so by starting a brewery in the grounds of the Abbey of Holyroodhouse in 1778. Although this was a traditional site for brewing as the monks of the old Abbey had always made their own ale, it was more Archibald's canny commercial sense that took him there. Beer brewed in the Abbey grounds escaped the duty of two pennies Scots that Edinburgh Town Council put on every pint sold in the city. A contemporary described Archibald's strong ale as 'a potent fluid which almost glued the lips of the drinker together and of which few could despatch more than a bottle'. It was popular in taverns, particularly in Johnnie Dowie's in Liberton's Wynd, where the young gentlemen of Edinburgh would gather in small windowless rooms, one a mere box jokingly called the

Abbey Brewery
c.1861.

THE ABBEY BREWERY THE PROPERTY OF MESSRS. W. YOUNGER AND CO.

Coffin, to celebrate Younger's Edinburgh Ale. Robert Burns was reputedly one of Dowie's customers.

By 1788 Archibald had a new brewery in Croft-an-righ, an ancient lane behind Holyroodhouse, his brother Richard owned a small brewhouse in Gentle's Close, off the Canongate, and William II, the youngest brother, was helping his mother run her Leith brewery.

In 1793 Archibald opened a new brewery in the North Back of Canongate, a site later merged into Waverley Station. The move brought him a fortune, as the new premises were larger, with better facilities and a well of good spring water.

In the same year as Archibald opened his new brewery his brother William opened vaults for the sale of ale and porter in Blair Street,

Leith. The earliest newspaper advertisement for ale, kept by the Scottish Brewing Archive in the University of Glasgow, dates from 1793. William placed it in the *Edinburgh Advertiser*, and it was simply one paragraph, introducing his new vaults. Three years later William had his own brewery, which, like Archibald's, had been set up within the Abbey's grounds. By 1803 he had bought James Blair's Abbey Brewery in Horse Wynd, which he developed so successfully that he was able to buy a country estate of 600 acres at Beattock, Dumfriesshire. To share the increasing workload, William took in two partners, his brother-in-law in 1808 and his brewery superintendent, Alexander Smith, in 1811.

Richard Younger, who had been quietly brewing in Gentle's Close, left

for London to become a partner in the brewing firm of Younger and Ryrie, his sister Jean having married into the Ryrie family. While there he invented, according to the patent, 'a new and improved method of extracting worts from malt, barley and other grains and substances'. Richard died in 1806.

In 1819 Archibald Younger, a bachelor, died, leaving everything to William who, after his mother's death in 1821, consolidated all the family interests under the name of William Younger and Co. He was 54 and since the beginning of the century had been steadily widening his market. Shipments to London through the port of Leith found a ready sale, and Younger carts were going as far north as Newburgh in Fife and as far west as Dumbarton.

After forming William Younger

& Co., William set about becoming Edinburgh's foremost brewer. In 1825 he bought an old house in the Canongate, once the town house of the Marquess of Lothian, named the Lothian Hut. Neighbouring ground followed and a building whose adjoining property he had leased with an option to buy in ten years' time. This gave William another small brewery, a coach house, a malt loft, a barn, a kiln, offices, houses and a well. All this was converted into the Abbey Brewery.

The growth in premises brought a commensurate growth in sales, and by 1830 Younger's strong ales were being dispatched throughout Scotland, reaching as far as Shetland and Orkney. The northeast of England was an important market, and even in London, where competition was fierce, the company was well established. By 1840 William was

Export label for Edinburgh Strong Imperial Ale made for Irving, Macarthur & Co., Demerara, British Guiana, South America.

exporting to the USA, Central and South America, most of the British colonies and the West Indies.

When William Younger II died in 1842, as did his partner Alexander Smith, their shares were left to their sons, William III and Andrew Smith, who had been made partners in 1836. The death of William was the last link between the great brewery in Edinburgh and the first humble brewery in Leith.

During the 1840s, under the direction of William III and Andrew Smith, trade grew rapidly, with special attention being paid to the United States market as the population there had risen considerably. The firm's New York agent wrote: 'The sale of Scotch Ale is increasing with us every year.' The United States was not the only export market to which attention was paid, however. The firm's letter records show that clippers were sailing from Leith loaded with Edinburgh Ale destined for the other side of the world. 'Ale should arrive during the open season from September to April' said a message from Bombay. From Port Adelaide came an urgent plea to 'miss no vessel from Leith'. The 1840s ended with the firm's notional centenary year (1849) and William III's eldest son, William IV, entering the brewery.

While during the 1850s the home trade expanded, Younger's products had become so popular overseas that they were being counterfeited. American customers in St Louis had to be warned against 'Yonkers', a pirate ale in the same kind of bottle on which, to escape prosecution for forgery, otherwise identical labels had 'Yonkers' substituted for 'Youngers.' Similar attempts by German competitors

Label for Younger's India Pale Ale bearing the company's triple pyramid trademark introduced in 1859.

were reported from South America. Younger was among the firms that supplied beer to the British troops sent to the Crimea in 1845 to help Turkey defend itself against Russian aggression.

The export trade certainly could be difficult. Consignments often arrived with the contents fit only 'for vinegar'. Slow voyages, shipwrecks, broken bottles, lost cargoes all had to be contended with. One cargo of forty casks lay for two years in Tobago before being sold. It was such a sturdy ale, however, that it was still in good condition, although too strong for local taste.

By the mid-1850s Younger's 'India Pale Ale', a clear, refreshing beer that kept and travelled well, had been introduced. It was popular in hot countries, and a New York importer was so disappointed at the non-arrival of supplies during the hot weather of June 1856 that he requested 300 casks 'without fail' by October and 300 by December. In Boston an importer had sold 100 casks so quickly that he wrote: 'We could have sold readily 500 casks of your ale.' As well as pale ales, Younger brewed strong ales and stouts of various qualities.

Younger's output came from one source – the Abbey Brewery. With sales soaring, however, a new outlet was required, and in 1858 the purchase of brewer Alexander Berwick's premises off Gentle's Close (the site of Richard Younger's brewhouse which Berwick had bought from him) enabled the construction of the Holyrood Brewery to begin.

Younger's fortunes during the last four decades of the nineteenth century fluctuated. The 1860s mirrored the 50s – increasing sales, additional premises, such as an office in London at St Paul's Wharf in Upper Thames Street. The 1870s were troubled, and by 1873 the company was in difficulties. There were problems with the uneven quality of the beer and dissent among the partners, with senior partner Henry Younger being accused of mismanagement. By 1878

sales had declined to the extent that partners' correspondence revealed concern over the 'bad times'. In fact, things were so bad that the company had to borrow £15,000 to meet immediate needs. The 1880s brought an improvement, and by 1883 the business had more or less recovered. The 1890s began with William Younger & Company becoming a public limited company.

A new century saw the company's premises still growing and its output amounting to one-fourth of the entire quantity of ale produced in Scotland. In 1903, however, the opening of a bottling plant in London was a disaster, leaving the company with 48,000 unused bottles.

When the Liberal government had no option but to withdraw its 1907 Licensing Bill because of massive by-election defeats and a rally in Hyde Park in 1908 attended by millions, it settled scores by massively increasing the cost of licences for public houses. This especially affected London, and as

Younger owned pubs there, by 1911 it had had to write off around £100,000 of its London loans. All was not despair, however, as an excellent summer and higher duty on spirits boosted beer sales.

The First World War severely affected the UK drinks industry. Apart from brewers losing their employees to the armed forces, they faced increased taxation, rising raw material prices, a reduction in supplies and restrictions on the sale of alcoholic drinks. As the war went on, worse was to come. With the country facing a dire shortage of food, in February 1917 the government banned barley malting and in May commandeered all stocks of unmalted barley. By then the price of beer had risen, which it did again in May 1918, the Chancellor of the Exchequer having increased the duty by 100 per cent, thus raising the price of beer from 20 to 50 shillings per barrel. The strength of beer was also reduced.

The 1920s began with Younger installing a plant for bottling chilled and carbonated beer, with products such as Sparkling Ale, Holyrood Ale and Scotch Ale making an appearance. These moves, however, coincided with a fall in drink consumption partly because of a revival of the temperance movement but mostly because of the high cost of a pint thanks to another rise in beer duty. To fight back, brewers improved their public houses and promoted new products. Younger did this by introducing 'Father William', the genial white-bearded old gentleman so long familiar in advertisements for his red waistcoat and yellow check trousers. Father William, plagiarised from Lewis Carroll's poem in *Alice in*

Holyrood Brewery c.1890.

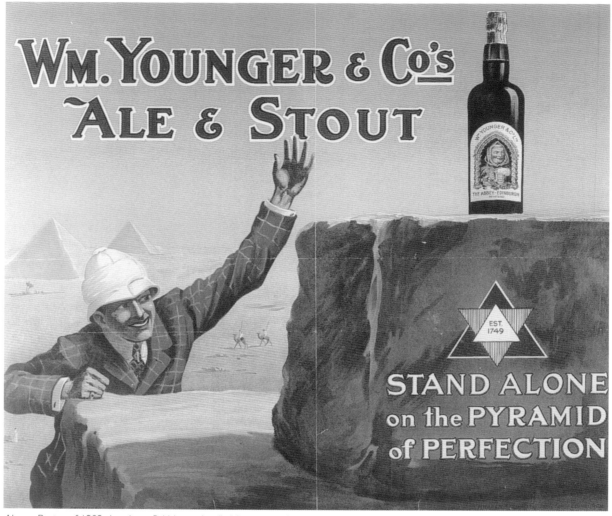

Above. Poster of 1909 showing a British tourist climbing a pyramid to reach a bottle of Younger's Monk Ale. The inspiration for the pyramid theme of the advertisement came from the company's pyramid trademark, prominently displayed.

Opposite. Younger showcard of the 1930s showing Father William pouring a bottle of Scotch Ale into a glass. The wording, 'Just what the Doctor ordered', would be challenged today by the Advertising Standards Authority.

*Wonderland*, first appeared in a press advertisement in 1921 with the couplet:

'You are old, Father William,' the young man did say,

'All nonsense, my lad, I get Younger each day.'

Father William's creator was artist Alfred Leete, who had produced the famous First World War poster that showed Lord Kitchener's finger pointing out over the caption 'Your Country Needs You'. Father William, first used on the label for Younger's new Sparkling Holyrood Ale, was registered as a trademark in 1927. When Leete died in 1933, Younger bought the copyright for Father William from his widow for £175. Included in posters created by Leete was the famous 'Old soldiers never die, they just get Younger every day'. In another poster Father William, with a pint in

Tavern signs

1930s' Younger pub signs. The one in the top right-hand corner hung outside Edinburgh's Holyrood pub and that in the bottom left-hand corner hung outside the Coach and Horses in Bruton Street, London, built in the early nineteenth century and given a mock-Tudor façade in the mid-1930s. Amazingly, during the Blitz the buildings on either side of the Coach and Horses were destroyed, leaving the pub intact.

McEwan-Younger Ltd, being formed to handle the joint export and naval and military trade of both firms. Although there was liaison between the two companies, they continued to operate in their own breweries and in most respects went their own ways. For example, Younger acquired more public houses in London, which, along with those it already had there, were refurbished in a mock-Tudor style. Such pubs were known as 'Scotch Houses', their Scottish association being emphasised by tartan draperies inside. Also refurbished were Younger pubs in other parts of the country. New artistic pub signs accompanied the refurbishments.

Having survived the Second World War, Younger celebrated its notional bicentenary in 1949 with the introduction of Double Century Ale, a 'spicy nut-brown ale' that was just as successful as Scotch Ale, introduced in 1920.

Although beer is still being produced under the Younger label, the Younger story really ended with its bicentenary for after that the company gradually lost its individuality and became part of a new story, that of Scottish Brewers which, when it merged in 1960 with Newcastle Breweries, became Scottish & Newcastle Breweries, now Heineken UK. Younger's famous Holyrood and Abbey Breweries are no more. Holyrood closed in 1985, with production being transferred to the new Fountain Brewery in Edinburgh, and the Abbey Brewery was cleared to make way for the new Scottish Parliament building. In spring 2004 it was announced that the Fountain Brewery would close.

*Information and illustrations courtesy of Scottish & Newcastle.*

his hand, was portrayed as Santa Claus.

In December 1930 came the announcement that Younger and one of its competitors, William McEwan, had 'negotiated a combination of certain of their financial and technical resources with a view to developing the efficiency of the production and distribution of their ales . . .' McEwan's had started in 1856. Its beginnings were modest, with a wages bill of 30 shillings, but growth came quickly and when the founder, the only William McEwan, died in 1913, the brewery in Edinburgh's Fountainbridge had become the hub of a worldwide sales network.

The new partnership, known as Scottish Brewers, officially came into being in 1931 with a subsidiary,

# GONE BUT NOT FORGOTTEN

## British Caledonian Airways

There are few people over the age of thirty-five who will not remember the TV commercials featuring the tartan-clad air stewardesses of British Caledonian Airways. 'I wish they all could be Caledonian girls' went the jingle inspired by the Beach Boys' song 'I wish they all could be California girls'. Featuring businessmen singing the words, the advert has been named as one of the best of all time. The passengers in the commercial sang:

'I've flown with US airlines, and the girls are really nice;

And those Far Eastern girls do splendid things with rice.

German girls are so correct, and the planes are never late;

But there's only one girl we want to see, as we reach the departure gate;

I wish they all could be Caledonian . . .'

The airline was proud of its Scottish image and, apart from its tartan-clad cabin crew, had the lion rampant emblazoned on the tails of its planes. It even had its own pipe band, and its posters often carried a picture of a piper at Edinburgh Castle. Newspapers and magazine campaigns featured the tartan-clad stewardesses with the phrase: 'Fly with Caledonian Girls'.

It is a shame that British Caledonian Airways, which disappeared when it was taken over by British Airways in 1988, is better remembered for its sexy TV campaigns showing girls in short tartan skirts than for how it came about, which is an astonishing story of how a working class lad from Glasgow made his mark, against all odds, on aviation history.

The founder of British Caledonian Airways, Adam Thomson, was the son of a shunter on the London Midland & Scottish Railway. He was educated at Rutherglen Academy, Coatbridge College and the Royal Technical College, now Strathclyde University. In 1944, when he was seventeen, he joined the Fleet Air Arm and was sent to Canada for pilot training. By the time he was demobbed he was a qualified pilot with aspirations to start his own airline. He therefore obtained a commercial pilot's licence, and two years after the war he and a partner acquired a Walrus biplane to fly mail to the fishing fleets and to give joyrides to holiday-makers at Largs on the River Clyde. While Thomson said it was a lot of fun, he could not get financial backing to keep Amphibian Air Haulage, as his company was called, going.

After Amphibian folded, Thomson had a number of jobs – as a pilot instructor with the Ministry of Civil Aviation, flying biplanes from the Isle of Wight to the Channel Islands for Newman Airways, working commercially with British European Airways and West African Airways, and transporting troops around Africa and to Singapore for the Britavia airline.

After seventeen years of working for other people, Thomson felt it was time to have another go at fulfilling his ambition – to have his own airline. Help in that quarter came from John de la Haye, who worked for Cunard Eagle Airways and was also planning to start his own airline as he thought the North Atlantic charter market was wide open for development.

Joining forces, the two men announced the formation of Caledonian Airways (Prestwick) Ltd

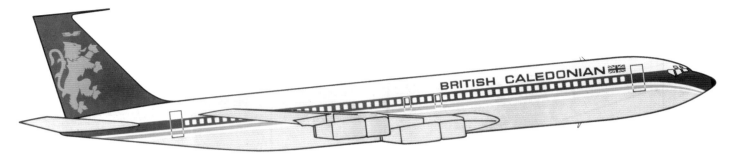

This drawing shows British Caledonian colours on a Boeing 707 used by the airline on all its intercontinental services and long-distance charters. The tail design represented the lion rampant of Scotland.

significant part of BA routes to B Cal in case it damaged BA's flotation prospects. After losing that fight, B Cal suffered other blows. Because of the Falklands War, it lost its Buenos Aires route. It lost Tripoli because of tensions with Libya, and fear of terrorism cut demand on North Atlantic routes. Economic chaos in Nigeria hit its Lagos service and, ultimately, in 1987, its lucrative helicopter service between Heathrow and Gatwick was halted on environmental grounds.

Meanwhile, having been floated on the Stock Exchange, BA was going from strength to strength and decided to end competition from B Cal by making a £235 million takeover bid for it. Although Thomson responded to the bid by inviting Scandinavian Airlines System to become a major shareholder in B Cal, an increased bid by BA won the day, and in 1988 the two airlines were merged, making the aviation world a duller place without British Caledonian's tartan livery.

Rather than sit on the board of the merged airline, Thomson retired at the age of sixty-one. It was a sad and bitter end to the story of a man of vision and courage who had made aviation history by building a place for British Caledonian among

the giants of the aviation world. That he had done it with little capital and with little help from government made his achievement all the more notable. Sir Adam Thomson died in 2000, aged seventy-three.

Although Thomson became a hard-headed businessman, he was an aviator at heart. In New York in the

1960s while negotiating a loan for new aircraft, he received an urgent call to say that the pilot of a B Cal New York-Bermuda flight had been taken ill. 'You're the nearest pilot, chairman,' said the caller. 'There's a uniform waiting in the cockpit.' 'So I flew the darned thing,' Thomson recalled, 'and I loved it.'

Advertisement for British Caledonian Airways' flights to Nigeria.

# DUNCANS CHOCOLATE

It is always sad when a company closes down, but it is even more so when, despite many setbacks and rebirths, it has survived for 142 years and in its heyday employed around 2,800 people. Such a company was confectioner Duncans of Scotland, which went into liquidation in February 2003. Generations will mourn the loss of their famous Hazelnut Chocolate Bar.

Duncans was a family business that started trading in 1861 when Mary Duncan and her eldest son, William, started a small retail cake business in Dundee where they made and sold homemade confections and dainty cream-topped cakes. Business flourished, and in 1884 they opened a shop at 205 High Street, Edinburgh. In the new shop, boiled sweets were made in the basement factory, and William Duncan soon gained a reputation for his high-quality confectionery. The best-known sweets were his glossy Satins (Raspberry Ices, Orange and Lemon Slices), Pralines and Fig Balls in their gold casing. (Such was the success of Pralines, that the name became the telegraphic address of Duncan's factory.) During the 1890s Duncan's sweets won many gold medals in international competitions.

In 1895 the business moved to Beaverhall Road where growth continued until, by 1916, the factory was nearly six times its original size.

William Duncan wanted to make Duncan's products as well known in England as they were in Scotland and in 1927 merged the company with Rowantree of York. He continued to be a director of Duncan, with Rowantree taking over responsibility for the further development of the business. Around this time William Duncan's son came up with the company's first chocolate and its most famous product, the milk chocolate Hazelnut

Hand-dipping chocolates In Duncan's Factory In 1918.

Bar, later symbolised in the Duncan trademark, which showed two busy little chefs roasting hazelnuts over an open hearth. After the Hazelnut Bar came Hazelnut Whirls, Walnut Whips, Chocolate Gingers, Capital Ginger Assortment, Parisian Fondant Creams and Orange Cream Bars.

In the 1930s, apart from its chocolate products, Duncan's range included Buttered Almonds, Bonbons, boilings, rocks, toffees and sweets known as 'Crisps' – lemon, blackcurrant, honey and butter, and mint – as well as old favourites such as Fig Balls and Satins. All these sweets were sold by weight from glass jars. Chocolates could also be bought by weight as well as packed in boxes.

Although by the 1950s Duncan was one of Britain's biggest exporters of confectionery, high advertising costs and stiff competition meant that by the 1960s it was no longer making a profit. Fortunately, however, Rowantree decided that, while it was no longer profitable to carry on the Duncan's business, the Edinburgh factory would be used to manufacture Rowantree products and most of Duncan's famous brands would be relabelled 'Rowantrees'. Thus, from the end of 1967 the Duncan factory was wholly concerned with the manufacture of Rowantree's Walnut Whip, and Dairy Box Assortment. Nutty Bars, Easter Eggs and bulk chocolate were also produced, and again the factory prospered.

Rationalisation of the Rowantree business saw the closure of the Edinburgh factory in 1987. With Rowantree's support, however, there was a management buyout, and it opened again shortly

'Join the Jocks'. An advertisement from what is believed to be an unused advertising campaign devised in the 1930s to publicise Duncan's Hazelnut Chocolate Bar. This one was intended to promote the product in England and offered an attractive enamel badge, featuring Hazelnut Jock, to every boy and girl on Tyneside who saved twenty-five wrappers from Duncan's Penny Hazelnut Bars.

afterwards as the new fully independent Duncans of Edinburgh. After an absence of twenty years Hazelnut Bars, Orange Cream Bars and Parisian Creams were back on the shelves under their original names. New products like Orange Curacao Bonbons, Apricot Brandy Truffles and Chocolate Ginger Pralines were launched.

Sadly, despite an encouraging start, the venture failed, and in 1991 the company was sold to Jeremy Salvesen. Apparently, he ate a bar of Duncan's Hazelnut every day, and when he heard that the company had gone bust, he bought it as he thought it ridiculous what had happened to the company that made the best chocolate in the world.

The new company, Duncans of Scotland Limited, moved to Motherwell Food Park, Bellshill, and from a start of only three different chocolate bars went on to produce

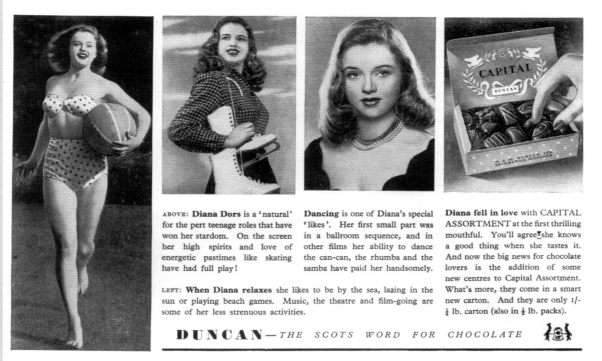

ABOVE: **Diana Dors** is a 'natural' for the pert teenage roles that have won her stardom. On the screen her high spirits and love of energetic pastimes like skating have had full play!

LEFT: **When Diana relaxes** she likes to be by the sea, lazing in the sun or playing beach games. Music, the theatre and film-going are some of her less strenuous activities.

**Dancing** is one of Diana's special 'likes'. Her first small part was in a ballroom sequence, and in other films her ability to dance the can-can, the rhumba and the samba have paid her handsomely.

**Diana fell in love** with CAPITAL ASSORTMENT at the first thrilling mouthful. You'll agree she knows a good thing when she tastes it. And now the big news for chocolate lovers is the addition of some new centres to Capital Assortment. What's more, they come in a smart new carton. And they are only 1/- ¼ lb. carton (also in ½ lb. packs).

**DUNCAN**—*THE SCOTS WORD FOR CHOCOLATE*

In the late 1940s and early 50s Duncan used British film stars to promote its Capital Chocolate Assortment. This advertisement shows a young Diana Dors, who was said to have fallen in love with Capital Assortment at the first thrilling mouthful.

more than 75 different products for both the home and export trade. An innovation by Jeremy was the Groovy Chocolate Card. Through the company's website, customers could design their own personalised card and have it printed on a 220-gram slab of chocolate. Edible ink was used to create the images on the chocolate. For £10 plus postage, the card could be made in either milk, dark or white chocolate, completely personalised and even incorporating photographs. An order placed one day would arrive in the post the next.

Unfortunately, history repeated itself, and in February 2003 Duncans of Scotland went into liquidation.

'Look! Duncan Hazelnut'. 1953 advertisement for Duncan's famous Hazelnut Chocolate Bar.

LOOK! DUNCAN HAZELNUT!

HEADS TURN, eyes brighten at the sight of Duncan Hazelnut. There's no resisting this smooth milk chocolate that's crammed full of hazelnuts. Every nut is skinned for extra sweetness, golden-roasted for fuller flavour. Enjoy it today—the good-time chocolate that *does you good*.

**DUNCAN**—*THE SCOTS WORD FOR CHOCOLATE*

# KLICK & MUNRO CLEANERS

Although, from Inverness to Penzance, Klick Photopoint and William Munro signs were familiar in almost every high street, most people who popped into the shops to have their photographs developed and their clothes cleaned had no inkling that Klick and Munro's origins lay in two rival laundry businesses in Glasgow in the second half of the nineteenth century. The rival businesses were those of the Bowie and Kennedy families whose descendants own the Bowie Castlebank Group, the owners of Klick and Munro.

As the Bowie and Kennedy businesses did not amalgamate until 1962, it is better to chart each family's operation before that separately, starting with the Bowie family who were the first to start up.

While the Bowie family's connection with laundry began with widow Annie Bowie going around factories with a wheelbarrow, offering to collect clothes for cleaning, it was her sons, William and John Bowie, who started a dyeing and scouring business some time between 1860 and 1861 at 59 Stevenson Street, Calton, in the east end of Glasgow. Two years later, the business had four branches, three in the east end and one on the south side. In 1870 the works moved to Strathclyde Street, Dalmarnock, creating the Clyde Dye Works. By 1879 there were thirteen branches and a new department, the Feather Room, where the dressing, curling and dyeing of feathers and feather boas was carried out. Feathers were high fashion at the time.

In 1882 William and John Bowie built and patented a steam-powered carpet-beating machine that was so successful that there was a demand for it not only in Britain but also on the continent and even in America. With the only means of cleaning carpets in the home being the broom, or switch, and tea leaves technique, it was a boon for housewives to be able to send their carpets to Bowie's for a beating. Indeed, it was one of the sights of spring-cleaning times to see the Bowie horse-drawn lorries piled high with carpets passing Bridgeton Cross in the evening on their way to the works.

While carpet-cleaning became the emphasis of Bowie's business, the dyeing department was kept busy. There was a year-round demand for clothing to be dyed black for mourning, and as fashions

The Clyde Dye Works, Dalmarnock.

W & J Bowie's patent steam-powered carpet-beating machine.

W & J Bowie dyeing and dry-cleaning shop in the 1920s.

did not change as quickly as now, instead of buying new clothing, people had their faded garments dyed.

*The Industries of Glasgow*, a book published in 1888, detailed W & J Bowie as 'Dyers, Cleaners, Carpet Beaters, Hot Pressers and Ostrich Feather Dressers'. The cleaning referred to was dry-cleaning, a reasonably new service introduced by the company. Dry-cleaning had been unknown until the mid-1860s when French tailor Jean Baptiste Jolly discovered the process accidentally. It was a luxury service used mainly by the wealthy whose womenfolk wore elaborate gowns and whose homes were filled with the latest in furniture, all seemingly draped with velvet or plush. When *The Industries of Glasgow* was published, W & J Bowie had twenty-three branches and 250 agencies in and around Glasgow. Customers, however, did not have to take their laundry and garments for cleaning and dyeing into a branch – there was a home collection and delivery service.

The years leading up to the First World War were productive for W & J Bowie. In 1907 the company opened a laundry in Carstairs Street, and in 1911 it participated in the Scottish Exhibition in Kelvingrove Park, Glasgow, where it displayed a beautiful green ball gown to advertise its dry-cleaning service. A fabulous display of feathers dyed to the various tints in the opal, a semi precious stone popular in engagement rings at the time, advertised dyeing.

During the 1914–18 war, the company found it difficult to keep going. As cleaning and dyeing was not considered an essential industry, there was a shortage of chemicals and dyestuffs. There was also a shortage of employees as the men joined the services. Transport was also a problem as at the beginning of the war, before mechanisation of the army, the company's fit horses were requisitioned.

Although the Bowie reputation was built on carpet-cleaning and dyeing, after the war the company leaned more and more towards garment-cleaning, its only formidable rival being Puller's of Perth, the first to start dry-cleaning in Scotland.

When the oldest company in the industry, Brand and Mollison, which had begun life in 1799 in Queen Street, Glasgow, was in trouble in the early 1920s, its chairman, Robert Stewart, asked John Bowie for help, which he did by becoming a director and sending one of his top men from the Clyde Dye Works to reorganise Brand and Mollison. Consolidation of the association between the companies

Cover for Bowie's house magazine of January 1949, which showed a cute Mabel Lucie Atwell cartoon character. BASL stood for Bowie's Associated Services Ltd, the registered company's working name.

Castlebank Steam Laundry horse-drawn collection and delivery van c.1890s.

This photograph from the 1920s shows a Castlebank window display of hats and garments that had been treated by the Franco-Barbe process. The remodelling of hats was big business in the 1920s and 30s.

came in 1923 when W & J Bowie became a private limited company with Robert Stewart as chairman and John Mollinson as a director.

Bowie introduced a innovative cleaning scheme in the early 1930s: the singling out for cleaning of essential wearing apparel – gents' suits, sports jackets, flannels and ladies' costumes – which, if received in the branches by 12 noon on a Tuesday, were guaranteed to be ready for collection on Saturday. While this might not sound like a big deal to us when we can hand garments in to be cleaned and get them back the same day, it was radical at the time.

During the Second World War Bowie worked to capacity cleaning and dyeing goods for the armed services, and as this work came under the Ministry of Supplies, cleaning and dyeing was recognised as an essential industry, unlike in the previous war. On the home front,

with clothes rationing and make-do-and-mend for everyone, civilian cleaning rocketed and the tight schedule, especially for the services' cleaning and dyeing, was a constant challenge.

Although, in 1952, Bowie had opened its first unit branch (cleaning done on the premises) at 202 Byres Road, Glasgow, following it with one in Clydebank, business was difficult as local entrepreneurs were eroding the traditional receiving-shop trade with their own on-site dry-cleaning. Action had to be taken, and in 1962 Bowie joined forces with a rival company, A. Kennedy & Sons Ltd of Anniesland, who owned the Castlebank Laundry. This created Bowie Castlebank – for both companies it had been either amalgamation or liquidation.

Now that the W & J Bowie story has been told, it is time to tell that of the company with which it amalgamated, A. Kennedy & Sons

Ltd, which began with Alexander Kennedy opening a furniture business at 404 Byres Road, Glasgow, some time around 1870. As well as being a cabinetmaker, upholsterer and furniture contractor, however, he also cleaned carpets and the heavy household furnishings and draperies so fashionable in Victorian days. The cleaning side of the business prospered, and on 7 August 1878 a factory was opened in Castlebank Street, on the site of the old Bishop's Castle on the banks of the River Kelvin in Partick. To signify the high quality of service that he aimed to offer the public, Alexander Kennedy introduced a trademark – a castle carried on the tail of a big 'C'.

Cleaning, dyeing and carpet-beating services were carried on in Castlebank Street until 1894 when they were moved to the cleaner air of Anniesland, at which time a laundry department was introduced.

Shortly afterwards, a research laboratory was added to explore the then novel coal-tar dyestuffs which enabled Castlebank to create every imaginable shade on every kind of textile, thus superseding the use of the older mordants and dyewoods.

In 1898 Castlebank inaugurated motor deliveries direct to their customers, a courageous step at a time when breakdowns were part of nearly every trip. Later, the fleet of yellow motor vans became so well known that they created the phrase 'Mother! Here comes the Castlebank man'. At the same time as motor deliveries were started, the first Castlebank branch office was opened in Glasgow, the forerunner of the sunshine shops which, with their fresh yellow curtains, were to be seen all over Glasgow and the west of Scotland.

Meanwhile, there came news that a French genius, M. Louis Barbe of Lyons, France, had created a unique process of dry-cleaning under absolute seal, without even the friction of air. Introduced into Scotland by Castlebank in 1908, the Franco-Barbe process, as it was called, was exclusively Castlebank's. In 1921 Castlebank extended the Franco-Barbe process to the cleaning, dyeing and remodelling of hats. The success of this service was put down to the Castlebank hat remodelling always being in the mode, the styles being selected by a leading fashion authority, Lady Victor Paget of New Bond Street, London.

While Castlebank encountered many of the same problems as W & J Bowie during the First World War, it marched on, and in its jubilee year, 1928, it inaugurated the Castlebank Valet Contract. Under this, £4 10s.

A 1920s' advertisement for 'Mother! Here comes the Castlebank man'.

This photograph, c.1920s, shows a convoy of lorries leaving the Castlebank factory to deliver a load of cleaned carpets.

worth of cleaning over the year was made available for £2 10s. It was a great boon to the customers and to the employees as it helped to balance employment throughout the year.

After the Second World War, life at Castlebank more or less mirrored that at W & J Bowie until by 1962 neither had an option but to join forces with its rival if they were to survive, neither company being able to compete with the introduction of home washing machines.

At the beginning of the amalgamation both businesses continued to operate separately, but gradually the work generated through the various branches was directed to the Anniesland and Maryhill factories until, by 1965, everything was based in these. By that time the company had pioneered the opening of coin-operated laundrettes in Glasgow, the first being set up in Alexandra Parade in 1962.

By the late 1960s it was realised that Bowie Castlebank had too many shops in decaying areas of Glasgow as redevelopment of the city shifted tens of thousands of people to new suburbs and towns. Worse still, not enough shops were doing dry-cleaning on the premises.

The solution was to buy the opposition so cleaning businesses such as Glens, Knox and Swiss were acquired. The major acquisition was the Ayrshire-based Munro Cleaners, under which name the company began trading.

Although Bowie Castlebank had expanded to maintain its dominance, the industry was in decline, and in 1975 the Castlebank Laundry at Anniesland was closed. By the end of the 1970s it was obvious that something had to be done to halt a decline caused by the decreased spending power of the Scottish population and also major changes in fabrics and fashions, with jeans, the 'crumpled' look and easy-care fabrics being the name of the game. The choice was clear – employ fewer people as Bowie Castlebank became a property company or diversify.

Diversification was chosen, and in 1981 the company bought a small photo-processing laboratory in Wishaw, which came along with the name Klick on three shops in England. The move, however, seemed doomed when just a few months later a major client pulled out, taking a third of the business in the process. In desperation, Bowie Castlebank decided to offer a

developing and printing service through its own dry-cleaning shops, and from then on there was no looking back for Klick Photopoint, as this side of the business became known as.

The photo-processing side of the business expanded very quickly with the purchase of small groups of shops in this type of business throughout Scotland, Northumberland and North Yorkshire and the opening of Klick shops farther south and in Wales, culminating with the purchase of larger chains – Photo-Processing based in Leeds and Max Spielman in Liverpool.

In December 2008, just a week after the famous high street names Woolworths and MFI went into administration, the Bowie Castlebank Group followed suit. The photo-processing business had been hit by the advance of digital photography, and the reduced number of clothes needing to be dry-cleaned had led to a contraction of the cleaning business which had all started with Annie Bowie taking in washing to make ends meet.

*Information and illustrations courtesy of the Bowie Castlebank Group.*

# SAXONE

Up until the early 1990s there was not a high street in Britain without a Saxone shoe shop. In fact, the name was possibly the most recognised in twentieth-century British shoe manufacture and retailing. It was a household name.

Although Saxone began in 1908, its origins lie in the firm of Clark & Sons, which began hand-making shoes in Kilmarnock in 1820 and had by the 1850s established an export trade with Brazil and Europe, the connection with Brazil having come about accidentally. Apparently, the Clarks were friendly with John Walker, the whisky blender, and when Walker found that a ship loaded with whisky bound for Rio de Janeiro had spare cargo space, he suggested to James Clark that he should fill it with a consignment of boots and shoes for sale 'on spec' in Rio. James did, and the Brazilians loved his footwear so much that he immediately established a retail outlet there. James Clark's son, George, expanded the Brazilian and European markets, and by the late 1890s forty retail outlets had been established in Brazil, from the Amazon to the Rio Grande do Sul.

When the Brazilian government imposed crippling restrictions on imported manufactured goods, profits dropped at Kilmarnock. Clark's answer was to build an extensive modern factory at São Paulo and formed Campanhia Calcado Clark of Brazil, which became the largest shoe manufacturer in Latin America.

As Clark's Kilmarnock factory at Titchfield Street (built in 1873) had manufactured all the footwear exported to Brazil, the building of the São Paulo factory left Kilmarnock's capacity exceeding the domestic and European markets. Alternative markets had to be found, and in 1901 Clark formed an association with brothers Frank and George Abbott of Northampton who had worked for the Manfield chain of retail shoe shops. As Manfield was a family firm and promotion prospects were doubtful, however, the Abbots started their own business, F. & G. Abbot. The association was mutually beneficial as Clark had manufacturing experience and factory capacity, the Abbotts British retail selling and merchandising experience. Both concerns

operated from Titchfield Street in Kilmarnock, with Clark supplying only men's footwear. Later, F. & G. Abbot sold the Sorosis brand of women's footwear manufactured by A. E. Little, Massachusetts, USA. Sorosis shoes were special in that they were made in various fittings, new to Britain. The name Sorosis was dropped some years later when it was pointed out that it sounded like the unpleasant skin ailment psoriasis.

Clark and Abbott sold their footwear under the trade name of 'Saxone' through which it became famous the world over for quality. There have been various explanations as to the origin of the name. One of the most far-fetched attributes it to George Clark's delight at Kilmarnock football club's 6–1 victory over a rival team and that when he heard the Kilmarnock supporters chanting 'sax-one, sax-one' he said 'That's it!' More plausible is the explanation that the name was originally meant to be 'Saxon', denoting ruggedness but when the trademark authorities decided that it had too much of a national flavour, the letter 'e' was added, forming the

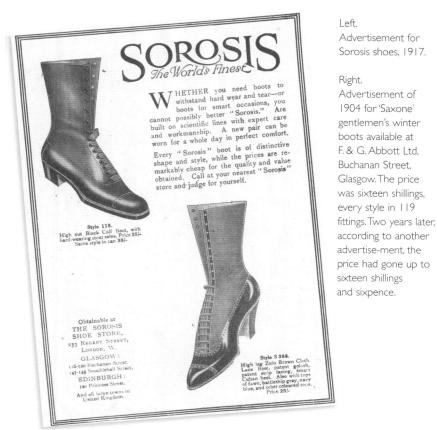

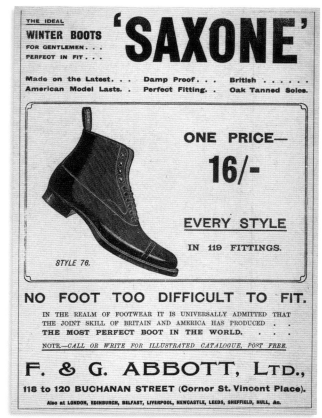

Left.
Advertisement for Sorosis shoes, 1917.

Right.
Advertisement of 1904 for 'Saxone' gentlemen's winter boots available at F. & G. Abbott Ltd, Buchanan Street, Glasgow. The price was sixteen shillings, every style in 119 fittings. Two years later, according to another advertise-ment, the price had gone up to sixteen shillings and sixpence.

word 'Saxone'. Whatever the explanation, Saxone became a household name for quality shoes.

The joint venture prospered, and in 1908 the two companies merged, creating the Saxone Shoe Company, with George Clark as chairman.

What gave Saxone the edge over its competitors was that, while other firms measured the length of the foot, Saxone introduced breadth fitting. It produced men's footwear in thirty half sizes with seven width fittings in each style, leading to the company's selling slogan, 'No foot too difficult to fit'.

Apart from selling from its retail outlets, Saxone sold from an illustrated mail order catalogue through which men in any part of

the world could secure Saxone shoes at factory prices and be certain that they would fit and wear well. The catalogue, which gave instructions for self-foot measurement, boasted that Saxone produced a shoe that was recognised by those who had tried it as the 'very best' while the cost was reduced to a minimum, making it possible to sell, with profit, 'a guinea shoe for the uniform price of 16/6'. Among the list of Saxone stores given in the catalogue were two in Paris and one in Brussels, which shows how far the company had expanded.

The Saxone Shoe Company's selling techniques were so successful that by 1914 it had 73 shops, by 1932, 114, and by 1939, 141. Even

the First World War and the Depression of the early 1930s had not stopped expansion.

In 1921 Saxone introduced a cheaper range of footwear under the label of Cable Shoes, the name being that of George Abbott's father-in-law, John Cable, who had introduced George Clark to the Abbott Brothers. C. & E. Lewis of Northamptonshire manufactured the Cable shoes. Although its manufacturing facilities expanded elsewhere, such as a factory in Gleneagles in 1949, the head-quarters of Saxone remained in Kilmarnock.

While the mainstay of Saxone was men's footwear, by the early 1950s it had become a leader in the women's fashion trade, and its

famous Jumping Jacks for children, made in Kilmarnock, were available throughout the UK as well as overseas. Saxone's golfing shoes, also manufactured at Kilmarnock, were unrivalled.

To protect its market position, Saxone amalgamated with Lilley & Skinner, which concentrated on women's footwear, forming Saxone Lilley & Skinner (Holdings) Ltd, a trading group with 470 retail outlets.

In 1962 Saxone, Lilley & Skinner acquired from Wolverine of America the UK franchise for Hush Puppies. Jack Abbot, chairman of Saxone, was convinced of the marketability of the strange new pigskin casual shoes and despite stiff opposition went into full production. He was proved right. An unprece-

dented advertising and sales campaign resulted in production not being able to keep up with demand and shoes had to be brought in from America.

In 1962 Saxone, Lilley & Skinner became a division of the British Shoe Corporation and remained so until 1988 when Sear, the holding company of the BSC, decided that the corporation should concentrate on sales and marketing. The manufacturing facility at Kilmarnock was therefore sold to Burlington International, which was given the exclusive right to manufacture products with the names Saxone or Hush Puppies in the UK and to sell them at home and overseas.

When the Burlington Group

went into receivership in 1992, Barratt Shoes acquired the Saxone brand, and while at first some shops remained trading under the Saxone name, eventually they vanished from the high street. Although the shops had vanished, shoes with the Saxone label were still available in Barratt shoe shops, but unfortunately these also vanished from the marketplace. The good news, however, is that in September 2003 Barratt launched a range of men's footwear bearing the Saxone label, so while Kilmarnock is bereft of its Saxone shoe factories, as are the high streets of Saxone retail outlets, the famous name lives on in the product in which it first started – men's footwear.

# STODDARD

## Stoddard CARPETS

A drawing of Arthur Francis Stoddard derived from descriptions of him. According to these, he was a short man, always dressed in black, with a tall hat and a big cigar. He was precise and correct and 'rather a terror' to those who worked for him.

Opposite. One of Stoddard's earliest tapestry carpets, woven in 1864.

Stoddard was Scotland's largest and oldest carpet manufacturer and an international name. The company held the royal warrant, and over the years had carpeted royal palaces, embassies, stately homes, luxury passenger liners, exclusive hotels and thousands of homes worldwide.

The founder of the company, American Arthur Francis Stoddard, an autocrat with a domineering temperament and a strong sense of social justice, was born in 1810 into a well-connected and wealthy family of British descent who had settled in Massachusetts in 1639. Stoddard began his working life with his uncle, Arthur Tappan, a silk merchant and importer of dry goods in New York. He must have done well as within a short time, he became a partner in the firm of Peter Denny, Importers, New York, which also had family connections. He was employed as its London representative, giving him the opportunity to travel both to Britain and to continental Europe.

Because of a slump in the United States that ruined his uncle's importing business, Stoddard left America in 1844, intending to set himself up in London as an agent catering to Americans and Europeans wishing to buy British goods. He was pessimistic about the future of the United States and considered its government less efficient than the British. In fact, so strong were his feelings that he later became a naturalised British subject.

Stoddard never made it to London. He docked at Greenock and made for Glasgow where he set up as a commission agent at Princes Square, 48 Buchanan Street. Whatever the reason for his change of destination, it was a lucky one, as A. & S. Henry, merchants and commission agents, Manchester, who were looking for a Glasgow outlet, appointed him their Glasgow partner. They made a wise choice, for the company soon had branches in Dundee, Belfast, Bradford and Huddersfield.

By the mid-1850s, Stoddard had moved from his house in Blythswood Square to Thornhill House, Elderslie. His passionate disapproval of slavery and the growing enmity between the North and South in the United States had decided him against returning home. 'He would not,' he said, 'live in a

Lion and Lioness. These picture carpets had a great vogue in the Middle East where they were in demand as part of a marriageable girl's dowry. They were not used as floor coverings but were prized as wall hangings.

country that called itself free and yet tolerated slavery.' Nevertheless, he visited America frequently and entertained his friends and relatives when they visited Scotland. (When, to him, the great day came that the North won the American Civil War Stoddard celebrated by giving a party at his Port Glasgow home for American friends during which he was said to have caused conster-nation to shipping in the Clyde by firing a twenty-one gun salute.)

While Stoddard decided to live in Britain rather than America,

thousands of people were doing the reverse – leaving Britain in search of prosperity and freedom in America. The nineteenth century had been beset by economic and political crises, and by 1852 Paisley's main industries, shawl manufacturing and silk weaving, had collapsed, killed by the cheaper materials woven on the new power Jaquard looms. The weavers and their families were starving, and charitable organisations chartered ships to take them to America for what they hoped would be a better life.

During the difficult times, Stoddard also found business slow as the American Civil War had brought with it a steady increase in duties. The Merrill tariff in the North raised duties from 21 to 35 per cent and Stoddard had relied on the North for business. He therefore decided to end his association with A. & S. Henry rather than suffer huge losses, and in 1862 he resigned from the partnership and retired from business.

Stoddard's retirement did not last long for within months he had bought Patrickbank textile mill in Elderslie, which had just closed down. It had belonged to brothers John and Robert Ronald who, in 1852, had begun producing block-printed Paisley shawls hoping to revive the market. They soon discovered this was impossible and switched to manufacturing printed tapestry carpets. This was also unsuccessful and the company was declared bankrupt.

Stoddard, who had met the Ronalds when he moved to Elderslie in 1853, offered to employ them. They, however, preferring a fresh start, refused his offer and, borrowing money from within their family, rented part of an empty Paisley factory. A relation by marriage, Peter Jack junior, joined them, and as he had not been involved in the bankruptcy, the new company was called Peter Jack Junior and Company. This time the company prospered, and by 1878 John Ronald had met his debts and the name of the company was changed to Ronald, Jack and Company.

Why Stoddard bought the business that was to be the foundation of the Stoddard carpet empire was vague, even to his son, Frederick, who wrote: 'What the inducements were to purchase is not clear as he knew nothing of the business.' Maybe he was bored with retirement and wanted the interest and challenge of a new venture? Whatever the reason, Stoddard set about developing his company, which he named the Glenpatrick Carpet Mills.

The original weaving shed held twenty-four people, but numbers rose quickly. Stoddard, with his business experience and connections as well as his wealth, succeeded where others had failed. Within five years he was selling three-quarters of the company's production in the United States, and when hostile American tariffs forced him to look for new markets, he found them in Europe.

In 1870, when Stoddard was sixty years old, he decided he did not want to spend all his time running the factory. He therefore brought into the company his son, Frederick, and Charles Bine Renshaw, who was born in Sussex and had come to Glasgow in 1870 on the staff of an East India house. He met Stoddard, joined the firm and a few years later married Stoddard's daughter, Mary. Stoddard still came to the factory two or three days a week and all his life took a keen interest in the progress of the business.

Stoddard took a practical interest in the social problems of the day. He was a supporter of William Quarrier, and in 1877 donated the first Quarrier cottage home, the Broadfield, named after his estate near Port Glasgow. Built into the cottage was a memorial plaque for his son Charles Noble Stoddard who had died while studying in Naples. Stoddard also presented Elderslie with its village hall and was instrumental in the establishment of Elderslie Public School.

When Stoddard died in 1882, Charles Renshaw became sole partner and in 1891 brought his brother, Arthur, into the business. Stoddard's son Frederick, who, like his father, was autocratic and inclined to disagree with his associates, had made little contribution to the development of the business and retired on his father's death.

Under the vigorous new management, the company expanded. New markets were found at home and abroad, and another factory was acquired, at Foxbar. In 1894 the firm was turned into a limited liability company with a capital of £350,000 – a large sum for a family business.

When Sir Charles Renshaw (as he had become) died in 1918, his brother, Arthur, became chairman. He, however, died a few months later.

One of Sir Charles last actions in 1918 was to bring the Caledonian Carpet Company of Stirling and Ronald, Jack and Company of Paisley into the Stoddard fold by an exchange of shares. The amalgamation with Ronald, Jack and Company had links with the past – it was the Ronalds' mill that Stoddard had bought in 1862, W. H. Ronald had become a director of Stoddard and Stuart Jack, part-owner and managing director of Ronald, Jack and Company, was the son of Peter Jack junior, who had helped the Ronalds make a fresh start more than fifty years before.

The Caledonian Carpet Company had been founded in 1875 and had carried on with varying fortunes. When the amalgamation with Stoddard took place its managing director was David Yellowlees, whose family were large shareholders.

Under the chairmanship of Sir Stephen Renshaw, son of Sir Charles, Stuart Jack and David Yellowlees successfully steered the group through the difficult days of the Depression of the 1930s and the Second World War, during which carpet-making was stopped. There was some weaving of other fabrics for war purposes, but most of the plant was dismantled and stored. The Paisley and Foxbar factories were closed and the Stirling factory was badly damaged during an air raid. Only the Elderslie factory was kept going, and it was converted into one of the largest laundries in Britain. Its purpose was to service convoys entering and leaving the River Clyde. Each week approximately 20,000 ships' blankets and 10,000 hammocks were washed and made up into regulation bedding sets. Also, 10,000 life jackets were washed and reconditioned each week.

When the Elderslie factory was reopened for carpet manufacturing in 1946, Stoddard began its greatest period of expansion under the chairmanship of Robert A. Maclean (later Sir Robert), who had joined the company in 1946 having before the war been a partner in James Templeton, the Glasgow carpet manufacturer. The expansion began in 1947 with the purchase of Douglas Reyburn, Kilmarnock, a woollen spinning mill. This was to safeguard raw material supplies. In the same year Stoddard's luxurious red carpet was laid down the aisle of Westminster Abbey for the wedding of Princess Elizabeth and Prince Philip.

Henry Widnell and Stewart of Midlothian became part of the Stoddard group in 1959. Inventor Richard Whytock, who patented the tapestry method of carpet production, had established it in Edinburgh in the early 1830s. (It was Whytock tapestry looms that Stoddard installed in his factory in 1862.) Whytock's inventions brought about such reductions in manufacturing costs that carpets began to be

Westminster Abbey with the Stoddard carpet laid ready for the royal wedding in 1947. Walter J. Bartram, the company's chief designer, painted the scene.

used for the first time in homes other than wealthy ones. Axminsters and Wiltons were the first types of fitted carpets. Axminsters were patterned and Wiltons plain.

In 1981 Stoddard Holdings acquired Templeton Carpets and Kingsmead Carpets. Rationalisation followed, with the closure of the Henry Widnell and Stewart manufacturing plant and then the huge Templeton manufacturing facilities. Kingsmead Carpets were sold in 1986. In 1988 Stoddard Holdings and Sekers International merged to form Stoddard Sekers

Opposite. Rock plants, alpines and garden flowers were the inspiration for this carpet design of the 1950s. It was one of many taken from natural surroundings.

International PLC. BMK was acquired in 1991.

In 2002 manufacturing at Elderslie ceased. This was because of a reduction in demand for traditional Axminster carpets as consumer preferences had moved towards less patterned and cheaper tufted products. Although the Elderslie plant was closed, a downsized Axminster operation was relocated to the company's Riverside plant in Kilmarnock. While in the past Axminster carpets were richly patterned, today most have understated designs set on a plain background.

Despite having a unique blend of high-quality design, traditional craftsmanship and the most advanced manufacturing technology, by the beginning of January 2005, mounting losses led to the company calling in the receivers. However, over-capacity in the UK carpet manufacturing section and overseas competition prevented a survival plan being put in place. Less than two months later the company ceased trading, and another of Scotland's great companies was no more.

As Stoddard's design library was one of the foremost collections of textile designs in the country, with beautiful hand-drawn illustrations and reference books covering every conceivable subject to stimulate the designer's imagination, the Heritage Lottery Fund awarded a grant of £18,700 to the University of Glasgow to begin work on preserving the archive. It has gained interest from around the world.

Information and illustrations courtesy of Stoddard.

# TEMPLETON CARPETS

**Templeton**

While the present generation might not be aware of the name Templeton in relation to carpets, previous ones have no difficulty in recognising it, for James Templeton & Co. was once the largest and most important carpet firm in the world. It was founded on the manufacture of chenille carpets, renowned for their softness, richness and beauty. To have one of these carpets was a status symbol, and people would speak with pride of their 'Templeton' carpet – not of their beautifully coloured and originally designed carpet, but of their 'Templeton' carpet. The name was more important than the colour or design.

The Templeton story started around 1820 when James Templeton, a farmer's son from Campbeltown, left home to work in Mr Rose's wholesale drapery business in Glasgow. Because of a decline in the drapery trade, however, he moved to Liverpool in 1823 and through a firm there obtained a lucrative post in Mexico. He was twenty-one years old when he left for Mexico, and when he returned to Britain three years later, he had savings of around £1,000 with which he intended starting his own business. Meanwhile, while looking around for the right opportunity, he began working for a Glasgow gingham manufacturer, and it was not until 1829 that he set up as a shawl manufacturer in Paisley, the Mecca of the world's shawl-making industry. No lady of fashion could be without a Paisley shawl. Their texture was the finest, their designs intricate and beautiful.

In Paisley, Irish weaver William Quiglay had been making shawls from round chenille, a velvety fabric originating in France and highly popular for curtains and table covers. Around 1837, while experimenting, he discovered that by steaming and pressing he was able to keep all the chenille tufts on one side, making them take the shape of a V with the cotton warps at the base.

Quiglay showed his findings to James Templeton who was

JAMES TEMPLETON
1802 – 1883

A rare sketch of James Templeton.

The Twelve Apostles Carpet laid out in the Stoddard car park in November 2003. The photograph shows just how large the carpet is when compared with the size of the cars around it.

astounded. Where round chenille was coarse, irregular and gave a fuzzy design, the new material was fine, smooth and gave a clear design. Not being reversible, however, it was unsuitable for shawls or curtains, and Quiglay had no idea what it could be used for. James Templeton, however, knew exactly what it was perfect for – carpets, where only one side was visible in use. By adding a solid backing to give weight and strength to the chenille, which on its own was a beautiful but flimsy piece of cloth, rich velvety carpets of any size and colouring could be produced more quickly and cheaply than traditional hand-woven Axminsters.

Templeton and Quiglay produced a sample rug that more than lived up to expectations, motivating them to apply for a patent. In 1839, with Templeton paying all the expenses, this was granted in the names of Quiglay and Templeton and gave protection for fourteen years.

James Quiglay, however, although an expert weaver was a simple man, and no sooner was the patent granted than he announced that he did not want to be a partner. He therefore allowed James Templeton to retain the patent's sole rights in exchange for a lump sum plus a guarantee of employment when manufacturing began. Six months later Quiglay sailed for America and was never heard of again.

James Templeton went on to set up a factory in King Street, Calton (now Redan Street), and started the first-ever manufacture of chenille carpets. When this factory burned down on Christmas Day 1856, he found new premises in William Street (now Templeton Street), and that was the beginning of what became the world's most famous carpet factory.

Templeton was world-renowned for its picture carpets, commissioned by the titled, the rich and the famous. Others were specially manufactured for exhibitions, like The Twelve Apostles Carpet for the Paris Exhibition of 1867. Forty feet by eighteen feet, it showed Christ standing on a pedestal with six Apostles on either side. The figures were taken from the famous statues by the Sculptor Thorwaldsen, which are preserved in Copenhagen. It is said that one of the weavers had a grudge against his foreman and deliberately inserted a wrong colour. This was not detected in the weft cloth, but when the chenille was set up to produce the completed carpet it was discovered that the Apostle Peter had bright blue hair! The carpet survives and is in the possession of Stoddard Carpets, which acquired the Templeton brand name in 1981.

Another Templeton picture carpet with a Biblical theme was one called Christ Blessing the Little Children, made for a Paris Exhibition of 1878. Such exhibitions were common during the days of the British Empire, with the government keen to display the country's wealth and manufacturing expertise to the world.

Apparently Mrs Abraham Lincoln, who was criticised for her extravagance in spending state funds

'Kirman' Abbey, a Templeton reproduction of an outstanding seventeenth-century carpet. The beautiful designs from Kerman (as it now is) in Iran were among the most highly esteemed of all Persian patterns.

Templeton's famous carpet factory in Glasgow Green, modelled on the Doge's Palace in Venice.

for the purchase of various articles, ordered 'a new carpet of Glasgow manufacture ingeniously made all in one piece, which had designs of fruit and flowers in vases, wreaths and bouquets'. Her 'extravagance' was not paid for until the end of the nineteenth century.

In 1888 Templeton acquired the patent for a spool Axminster loom, a development of the Skinner loom in America. Thirty looms were ordered and the famous Albert Mill facing Glasgow Green was built to house them. Started in 1889 and modelled on the Doge's Palace in Venice, it is one of Glasgow's most exotic buildings and is such an architectural landmark that it featured on a stamp when Glasgow

was the European City of Culture in 1990.

During the 1920s Glasgow-born architect, artist and designer Charles Rennie Mackintosh and his wife, Margaret Macdonald, collaborated with Templeton on innovative and original textile designs, later known internationally as 'The Glasgow Style'.

The demise of Templeton started when it bought Grays of Ayr in July 1969. This put such a financial strain on Templeton that a couple of months later it accepted an offer from the Guthrie Corporation, a rubber and palm oil organisation that wanted to buy into the carpet industry. Unfortunately, Guthrie, trading under the name of British

Carpets, was not knowledgeable about carpet manufacturing and that, coupled with a downturn in the industry, meant that Templeton did not make a profit, and in 1981 it was taken over by Stoddard Carpets, which closed its manufacturing facilities.

While Templeton's carpet factory might have ceased production, people still talk about Templeton carpets, as the name was a byword for quality. In fact, such was the quality of the carpets that many people still have them in their homes looking almost as good as new.

*Illustrations courtesy of Stoddard Carpets.*